T0383412

Anna Maria's

BLUEPRINT
QUILTING

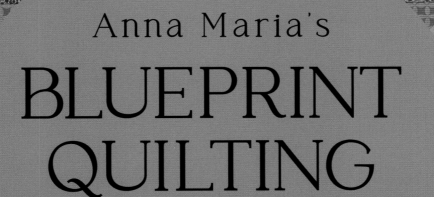

Anna Maria's
BLUEPRINT
QUILTING

Explore Color, Pattern, and
Technique with 16 Joyful Projects from
4 Simple Design Structures

ANNA MARIA
PARRY

QUARRY

Quarto.com

© 2025 Quarto Publishing Group USA Inc.
Text, Photos, Illustrations © 2025 Anna Maria Parry

First Published in 2025 by Quarry Books, an imprint of The Quarto Group,
100 Cummings Center, Suite 265-D, Beverly, MA 01915, USA.
T (978) 282-9590 F (978) 283-2742

All rights reserved. No part of this book may be reproduced in any form without written permission of the copyright owners. All images in this book have been reproduced with the knowledge and prior consent of the artists concerned, and no responsibility is accepted by producer, publisher, or printer for any infringement of copyright or otherwise, arising from the contents of this publication. Every effort has been made to ensure that credits accurately comply with information supplied. We apologize for any inaccuracies that may have occurred and will resolve inaccurate or missing information in a subsequent reprinting of the book.

Quarry Books titles are also available at discount for retail, wholesale, promotional, and bulk purchase. For details, contact the Special Sales Manager by email at specialsales@quarto.com or by mail at The Quarto Group, Attn: Special Sales Manager, 100 Cummings Center, Suite 265-D, Beverly, MA 01915, USA.

10 9 8 7 6 5 4 3 2

ISBN: 978-0-7603-8906-5

Digital edition published in 2025
eISBN: 978-0-7603-8907-2

Library of Congress Cataloging-in-Publication Data

Names: Parry, Anna Maria, author.
Title: Anna Maria's blueprint quilting : explore color, pattern, and
   technique with 16 joyful projects from 4 simple design structures / Anna
   Maria Parry.
Description: Beverly, MA, USA : Quarry Books, 2025. | Includes index.
Identifiers: LCCN 2024028015 (print) | LCCN 2024028016 (ebook) | ISBN
   9780760389065 (board) | ISBN 9780760389072 (ebook)
Subjects: LCSH: Quilting--Patterns. | Patchwork--Patterns.
Classification: LCC TT835 .P35187 2025 (print) | LCC TT835 (ebook) | DDC
   746.46/041--dc23/eng/20240625
LC record available at https://lccn.loc.gov/2024028015
LC ebook record available at https://lccn.loc.gov/2

Design and page layout: Megan Jones Design

Printed in China

This book is dedicated to the most gracious
educators who helped me figure out who I am
and what I have to offer the world. They also taught
me how to teach, and I am eternally grateful to them.

Flowerree (Galectovic) McDonough, Doris Carter, and Marcia Goldenstein

---

ACKNOWLEDGMENTS

I want to thank my family and my husband, Vince, for their support
of me and my creative ambitions. Life is so splendid when you
have people that completely understand and love you.

A huge thank-you to Melissa Kelley of Sew Shabby Quilting for her
amazing work on all of my machine-quilted quilts. Her spirit and
quickness have been a joy to have along for the ride.

Having Juliana Horner's skilled eye on the other side of the
lens for every photograph makes this book all the more
beautiful for the reader and so special for me.

CONTENTS

PART 3

The Blueprints 63

INTRODUCTION

I vividly remember the moment my art school watercolor instructor, Marcia Goldenstein, introduced me to the work of Jennifer Bartlett, who spent three years studying and drawing a single garden in the same location, over and over again: mountains of artworks, many of them the exact same scene, but each so very different. My mind was frenzied with the thought of such a lovely yet challenging venture. Could I repeatedly make one scene interesting? What would it entice me to create which might not have ever been created if I only engaged the view once? *I could make so much*, I decided.

I was so captivated by this idea that it effectively embedded itself as a code within me to explore as much as I could. To overlook boredom and replace it with curiosity. To trust that every attempt, even at the same endeavor, is a new opportunity to tell a story of beauty.

There is no known quilt maker in my family. While there is plenty of handcraft history that I have carried on in various forms, and even written books about, I was always most interested in making art. Throughout fine art school, I became familiar with what could happen within the four corners of a canvas long before I can remember seeing the four corners of a patchwork quilt. I therefore first viewed the quilt space as an invitation to make something happen like might happen on a canvas, albeit with fabric and considerably less spontaneity of process.

My first artistic relationship with quilt making was designing fabrics for quilt makers, which I have been doing since 2005. While I did understand that most people who purchased my fabrics would be making quilts, I did not anticipate becoming a quilter in the sense that I think of myself now. Would I make some quilts? Sure. But over two decades, I feel more that the quilts have made me.

I have spent many years teaching myself traditional techniques, practicing my own versions of various methods, amassing a knowledge base of blocks, exploring exciting palettes, and sharing my design point of view with quilters all over the world. However, I feel I have found my personal voice in patchwork primarily through my use of structure; in other words, how the quilt space is composed as a whole, beyond a simple and common exercise in repetition. I have realized that I build my ideas for my quilts first from an overall architectural vision of sorts, then the details of color, print, and value are all secondary in the process.

Further, I have found that there are certain aesthetic compositions or "blueprints" of quilts I've made where creating it just once did not satisfy my curiosity. Changing techniques, altering color palettes, and adjusting piecework scale entertains me, but all the while with confidence in the result due to working within a familiar structure. Just as you can keep the basic footprint of a house the same but completely change the look and feel by how you develop each space within it, you can remodel a quilt structure with an exciting new result each time.

It is from this structural point of view that I am excited to uncover my process for you, with plenty of variety in skill level so that you can pick the most comfortable starting place. After a brief stopover in Art School and Patchwork School, this book shares the patterns and instructions for four of my most reliable quilt structures and adaptations of each.

So, with my first book on quilt making, I'm thrilled to encourage your patchwork journey from this unique perspective with the hopes that your confidence and excitement for quilt making grows. My greatest hope in writing this book is not that you make quilts more like me, but that you make quilts *even more like you than you ever have*. I am so honored to help.

Art School

1

If you're a quilter, you're no doubt already an observer of your environment. Where others see tiled floors, you see quilt blocks. Falling in love with a flower could inspire your next appliqué adventure. I am no different than you.

This visual and tactile leaning that I was born with led me to only ever consider studying art formally. In art school I was able to intentionally devote time to developing my ideas and exploring the outer reaches of various mediums with those ideas. I look back now, thirty-three years later, and see that time in my life as sacred.

As a quilter, I realize that art school taught me how to be a quilter with classic elements of art, composition, and narrative. In this chapter, I want to share an overview of those elements that continue to inform my choices when I am making quilts. In some cases, I will translate art language into quilt language so that we can directly apply it to the projects in this book.

I offer these considerations with a genuine love for art and design. In short, welcome to my personal art school crash course for quilters.

BRAVING THE ELEMENTS: THE ELEMENTS OF ART

All visual art, whether a weaving or an oil painting, can be broken down into various elements that contribute to the overall visual expression. Depending on which art theory book you're reading, the number of elements can vary. I will share what I consider to be the core seven elements of art as they relate to all visual media.

1. COLOR

Color is perhaps the most translatable element from the art world to the quilt world. The fascinating (and potentially daunting) thing about color is that we all see it a little differently. Not to worry! There is a science to how the spectrum works in relationship to itself. Sir Isaac Newton was the first to create the circular diagram that we call the color wheel, and there is no handier tool to have on hand when choosing a palette.

We frequently hear the *temperature* of a color referenced, such as how "warm" or "cool" it is. Visually speaking, warm colors tend to come forward, and cool colors tend to recede. Every single color in the rainbow can have a warmer or cooler version of itself. In my experience, once we familiarize ourselves with color categories, it is the color wheel that can teach us simple formulas for beautiful combinations.

COLOR CATEGORIES

The first and most simplistic category of color is primary, which is made up of red, yellow, and blue. All colors are derived from various combinations of these three hues. While the three colors next to one another look more like a national flag than a work of art, the simplicity of the primary combination can simultaneously evoke postmodern art (think Miró) and 1930s ditsy floral prints.

Life gets more interesting as we introduce the secondary colors of orange, green, and purple. They sit between the primary colors on the color wheel and exist by way of primary combinations. As you no doubt learned at a young age, red and yellow create orange and so on, as you move around the wheel.

The third category of color is tertiary. The tertiary colors are created when you combine a secondary with a primary color and they sit in between them on the color wheel. So orange combines with yellow to become yellow orange. These more nuanced colors offer us lovely depth and interest.

▶ *With so many fabrics to choose from, patchwork is an exciting way to explore the color wheel.*

COLOR FORMULAS

Let's look at the behavior of colors in their purest forms. The following formulas can help you create harmony and excitement with a few simple tricks.

Analogous

If you're looking for a harmonious color scheme, pick a favorite spot on the color wheel and look no further than the color to your left or right. For instance, if you want an easygoing blue palette, you could include blue, blue-green, and green. With this scheme, you have primary, secondary, and tertiary colors all in one palette. It really is as simple as it seems. This is a stress-free and joyful exploration of hue when you're selecting fabrics for a project.

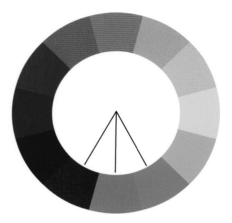

Analogous

Complementary

Should you desire a bit more drama or fullness in your palette, start with any color, then look directly across the wheel to find its complement. In the simplest sense the complement is the exact opposite. And because the opposite hue will create visual tension, it is a wonderful place to start developing a full color palette. In choosing a quilt palette, these color duos can travel through many fabric versions of themselves to create a rich variety. The Hedgerow Quilt (page 73) is a lovely exploration of the green and red color story, which includes aqua and coral shades.

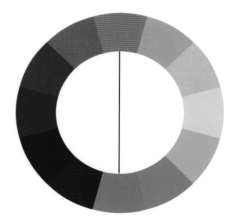

Complementary

These fabrics are ready to create a stunning quilt with a harmonic triad color formula.

Harmonic Triad (or Split Complement)

One of my favorite tricks in the complement game is to not choose the direct opposite but replace it with the hue to the left and right of it. So instead of using an obvious yellow/purple combination, I choose yellow, red purple, and blue purple. When I'm "fabric shopping" in my studio, using these tertiary colors on either side of purple invites magentas, pinks, lilacs, and lavenders to the cutting table. All this variation will create interest but keep the same yellow/purple identity that is appealing.

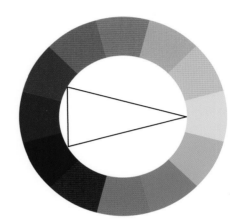

Harmonic triad

Tetrads (or Double Complement)

Another palette-building trick places either a square or a rectangle within the color wheel to yield a four-color scheme. The four corners of a square will point to a palette that includes two complement pairs. So blue and orange alongside yellow and purple is a tetrad scheme. One benefit to this sort of palette is that no one color is especially dominant, but rather it is full of character and interest.

I have never thought of these formulas as rules as much as good reminders of what to try when playing around. There is a lot to be said for going with your gut.

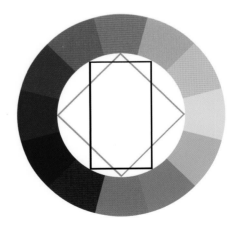

Tetrads

2. VALUE

When we use the word "value" to describe color, we're referring to how light or dark it is. Some colors are naturally lighter than others in their purest forms. For instance, yellow is intrinsically a lighter value than purple. However, if we set orange, red, and green next to each other to compare their light and dark qualities, they may all appear not especially light or dark but similarly medium in their value. As you may have guessed, value is relative.

In painting, the same color of orange can experience countless versions of itself by adding white to make it lighter (tinting) or adding black to make it darker (shading). You can create even more subtle versions of color by mixing gray (both black and white) to create "tones."

Value in and of itself becomes an extremely important tool in visual art. Choosing an overall very dark or very light palette can set the mood instantly. If your entire quilt is made up of medium tones, it could be extremely colorful yet "mushy" without the contrast of light and dark.

Consider the Time Travel Quilt (page 163). The background gradually moves from light to dark gray tones. The colorful twisting bias loops gradually move from light to dark as well but they do so in the opposite direction so that they show up well on the background. However, in the middle of the quilt we have medium-value colors against medium-value gray backgrounds, so the lines meld into the background a bit.

Anna Maria's Blueprint Quilting

3. LINE

The element of line is fundamental to all art. In drawing and painting, lines often describe what we are looking at. They do so by defining shapes with various thick, thin, faint, heavy, or lively marks. In a quilt, an appliquéd vine is the path from which a beautiful array of flowers and shapes can grow. Lines lead our eyes around a space almost like arrows telling us where to look.

Line can be implied. In other words, a patchwork quilt that is only made up of squares will still have elements of line that are apparent depending on the color, value, and arrangement of the squares, such as if several of the squares are blue and, in a row, there is a line. Our often-unintentional lines are sometimes very defining when we view our work from a step back. And frequently this step back inspires a rearrangement of elements if the "line" is not pleasing to us.

In the Terrace Views Quilt (page 113), there are literal scalloped lines that define the center of the quilt. Yet even if these echoing vines were absent, the same scalloped lines would be implied by the organization of the curved fan block rows on both sides of the quilt.

4. SHAPE

No one does shape like a quilter; we have that element of art down pat. And while classic art shapes can be anything from circles and ovals to squares and rectangles, quilt makers use every version of star, diamond, hexagon, pentagon, octagon, and then some. Most of the time the shape boundaries tend to be the actual lines of construction between pieces of fabric.

It is the combination of shapes that define patchwork as an art form. In other words, a collection of similarly colored triangles can arrange themselves to create an oval. I feel this visual endeavor gives the viewer something to appreciate up close as well as from afar. The Kiss on the Lips blueprint projects beginning on page 127 celebrate the shape of an *X* through more or less obvious patchwork renditions. So don't overlook stepping back to take in the overall effect of your arrangement to be sure you appreciate any intentional or unintentional shapes that have evolved.

5. FORM

The element of form takes shape to another level, and in sculpture it takes it to a third dimension. The three-dimensional form reveals itself to us with its size, volume, height, and width.

When we're speaking about form in a two-dimensional space, like a canvas, we're really talking about creating an illusion of form in space. This often employs various techniques of highlighting, shading, color, and perspective to convince the viewer that we are looking at an object that occupies an area. For instance, a vase of flowers that casts a shadow and appears glassy, because of the highlights depicted on the rim, is an illusion of a shape in space.

When we are talking about form in quilts, it might conjure the idea of pictorial quilts, such as a row of flower vases with appliquéd blooms popping out of the top. While a quilter might not necessarily try to create the illusion of reality with patchwork vases, giving the piecework on the vase a darker side and a lighter side can convey some shading.

There is a dazzling array of repetitious optical illusion quilt patterns that are simpler to construct than they appear. Further, physical form can be created with appliqué, and quilting, to create shadows and form in the actual material manipulation of the quilt as an object.

6. SPACE

The final element of art to share is a sort of setting where all of the other elements happen: in a space. Space, in art terms, is the idea that all the forms that we are looking at exist within the confines of the canvas, or image space.

Speaking simply, space can be defined by how objects are arranged or styled. The physical organization of space, whether it is predictably repetitious or chaotically unpredictable, can evoke emotions before you even have a moment to take in the construction, the forms, or the colors. Judging space more basically for its layout styles might speak to us more tangibly as quilters. Is it cluttered, vast, organized, symmetrical, or asymmetrical?

7. TEXTURE

In art we are not just convinced of objects in space being real enough to reach out and touch, but we are also anticipating what the objects would feel like in our hands. Whether it feels rough, smooth, soft, or bumpy all depends on how the object is depicted in the artwork. Texture is not always implied with visual tricks of artistry, but sometimes it is because the actual surface of the artwork is textured in some way.

In quilting, our texture opportunities are also bridged between the visual and actual. Visually, much of the perceived texture in a quilt has to do with the appearance of the fabrics that we choose and the style of printed fabrics, if we are using them. For instance, soft watercolor prints will have a different perceived texture than very bright and harshly colored graphic prints.

Further still, we can create texture in our quilts through many different styles of quilt stitches and the loft (thickness) of the batting we use.

Conversations with Georgia (page 169) has abundant textural interest through using diverse fabrics as well as an organic machine-quilting style featuring cursive writing.

"PRINCIPLES" OFFICE: THE PRINCIPLES OF COMPOSITION

isual composition is essentially the arrangement of the elements in the artwork. Composition has seen various ideals or rules evolve over the centuries in terms of what is thought to be perfect or most pleasing to the eye. And as you might expect, various rules have been developed and subsequently ignored over and over again throughout art history. We can look at every period of art and each of their ideals as inspiration for our compositions. All of these, often conflicting, rules that have been heralded throughout the ages offer us exponential directions for design. So, at once there are no rules and there are countless rules—take your pick!

Why is composition important? An artist can be an expert at painting the human face to look believably real; however, if the figure is composed onto the canvas in an imbalanced way, it might distract you from appreciating the perfect rendering. The same can be true for the work of an expert quilter. Their appliqué technique can be incomparable, but if the elements are visually out of balance and cause the viewer to only look at one spot of the quilt, something is amiss. Your creative efforts deserve to be displayed in the most pleasing composition possible.

This book presents a collection of quilt projects that are defined by their architectural attributes and therefore categorized by their compositional features. Again, the number of these principles varies depending on your source, but I am presenting seven. It is important to keep in mind that a single composition does not have to be an example of all principles, but in many cases these principles work together to help you achieve clarity of vision.

1. BALANCE

Balance refers to an equal disbursement of elements in a visual space to create a sense of formality or even calm. Traditional patchwork, by its very nature, offers a multitude of ways to achieve balance with the layout of regular and repeating block styles. The balance can be achieved through color, value, line, and shape. Even when there are no set "blocks," you can create balance.

SYMMETRY

Symmetry is the most formal of all ways to achieve balance. Symmetry happens when the elements on the right and left of the composition are identical and mirror each other. This naturally draws the eye toward the center and offers a sense of stability.

RADIAL SYMMETRY

Radial symmetry creates more than a symmetrical balance on the left and right, but also toward the top and bottom. In other words, each quadrant of the composition is identical in its arrangement. The Open Borders Quilt (page 141) is a perfect example of radial symmetry. The center holds the attention, and the design of the four corners radiating out are of equal importance as they all mirror each other in the layout of color, shape, and value. Many, but not all, medallion-style quilts, such as those in the Grand Central Blueprint chapter (page 65), have radial symmetry as their composition style.

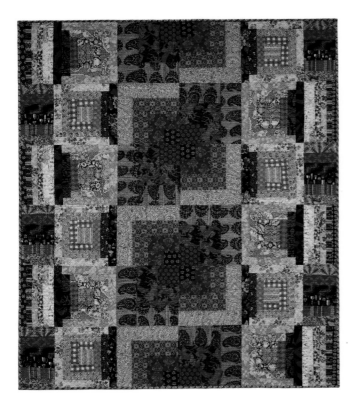

The organization of the Roman Numerals Quilt (page 97) illustrates symmetry. Not only do the shapes of the appliqué pieces repeat each other on each side of the quilt, but the colors of those pieces are identical on each side as well.

ASYMMETRICAL BALANCE

Elements do not have to replicate each other or be perfectly equal in a composition in order to achieve balance. An asymmetrical composition can feel balanced when the elements carry a generally similar weight on each side of a composition. For example, one larger element can be balanced by several smaller ones. The Conversations with Georgia Quilt (page 169) exemplifies an asymmetrical composition. The central bursting design moves with some organic strips and curves, but keeps an overall sense of balance.

2. FOCUS & EMPHASIS

As noted in the descriptions of different types of balance, compositions will often create a layout that encourages the viewer to look in one place, or at least to look there first. And frequently there are supporting roles taking some focus and emphasis in a composition as well. Take the Kaleidoscope Quilt (page 129) into account. The blocks of bright yellow, pink, and red are the first thing that hold your attention as they are centrally placed and contrast the surrounding deeper colors.

Emphasis can be created not just through color but also through value changes and how crowded a space is. If you give one element, whether in the center or off-center, a lot of blank space to move around in, then it will draw attention to itself.

3. MOVEMENT

Movement in composition evokes a pathway of portrayed or implied motion taking place in a scene. Portrayed movement can be the behavior or pose of various elements in the composition. For instance, perhaps a figure or animal is shown in motion, like a running horse or a speeding train. Colors, gestural strokes, and the direction of drawn lines can help to evoke this. But also, the overall structure of a composition encourages the idea of movement. A curving or angled road that moves diagonally from side to side on a landscape takes the viewer's eye with it as it travels from the foreground of the painting toward the far-off distance.

The movement created in the Spontaneity Quilt (page 81) carries your eye from the lower center of the border and up both sides to land in the garden of appliqué on the top border.

4. REPETITION, PATTERN & RHYTHM

I am always delighted when I see artists using the principles of repetition and pattern in their works, as not all artists do. I especially love seeing a printed dress or interior detail portrayed with a lot of attention and care; I feel the artist is speaking my love language of print. There are differences, at least in art terms, between repetition and pattern.

Repetition is really a less regular cousin to pattern. Repetition can be illustrated by the entire scene of lilies in Claude Monet's *Water Lilies*. The lilies do not appear regularly in their spacing or color, but organically as they would in nature. However, the retelling of the same form carries a reliable dotting of detail across the canvas.

The work of Gustav Klimt, or even Frida Kahlo's self-portraits in traditional dress, would be excellent resources when studying pattern in artwork. The patterns painted in their work depict clothing, lace, or other adornments. They look organic, but they carry a more regular quality and texture like textiles that we are familiar with in some way.

Patchwork sits right at the center of repetition and pattern. So much so that there is hardly any meaningful advice to offer in including these principles in your quilts, as these principles *are* your quilts. One suggestion that I will offer is to perhaps use these principles in less obvious ways. For instance, any block-style quilt will offer repetition and pattern by default. While the Time Travel Quilt (page 163) appears to be a block-style quilt, it is really no such thing. There is a regular patchwork of twenty gray squares in the background; however, there are no repeats of the same fabric recurring regularly.

The direction of repeated lines can change course as in the Fence Line Quilt (page 105). Changing the rhythm of a pattern can encourage one to break out of patchwork norms.

The principle of rhythm is often included alongside repetition and pattern, and that is simply when the style of pattern carries a very reliable space between elements. In other words "proximity" of the pattern is predictable. And like any song, that rhythm can change along the way to create some variety. The color can change, the value can change, and the quality of the line can change.

5. VARIETY, HARMONY & UNITY

Variety and harmony in art are at opposite ends of the same principle. Variety offers us the cure for sameness, and harmony keeps us from getting overwhelmed or bewildered trying to decide where to look when viewing artwork with too many disjointed parts. Unity is the overall feeling of oneness in an artwork that offers cohesion. You might even say that unity offers the feeling that the work is complete and whole.

The simple task of finding multiple shades of a single color to include in a quilt that has regular positions to feature the color is the definition of implementing variety (in the various fabrics) and harmony (in the color used). Consider the Terrace Views Quilt on page 113. The fan blocks on the left and right vertical borders play out various shades of pink and coral in a way that keeps the blocks from ever repeating themselves exactly. So, there is variety in the print styles and specific hues of pink and coral, but there is harmony in the repeating patchwork shape.

There are so many ways to achieve variety and harmony in our quilts beyond color. A more unexpected way is to let some patchwork forms repeat themselves in a different way altogether, such as through scale and style of print.

6. SCALE & PROPORTION

Scale as a principle is not just the size of the artwork itself, but also the size of it in relation to the human body. Our experience with art is very different when a work is small compared to when it is large. The scale of the piece itself has a certain amount of impact, either overwhelming or presenting itself as small and therefore seemingly fragile. In terms of quilts, we think about scale as a way for the quilt to function as a utilitarian item on a bed, couch, or crib. But we also think about them functioning simply as works of art for our walls.

In addition to scale referencing the size of the piece as it relates to us, scale is considered in terms of the size of various shapes within the work in relationship with one another. In a work of art, we would traditionally consider the larger elements to be the more important ones, or what the artist wants us to spend the most time engaging. Manipulating scale is an interesting way to create narrative in art.

Proportion is the relative scale of smaller units that make up one large unit. For instance, if we use time-honored human size relationships between nose, mouth, and eyes, we can create a more realistic rendering of the face. Proportion is not really something that we consider for quilt making, and where it does apply, we would really be speaking about balance and variety in scale.

7. CONTRAST

I will admit to saving what I believe is the best for last. Perhaps one of the most fundamental principles in composition is contrast. No contrast would be like having a month of night or a month of day—where is the joy? If it is your hope to engage the viewer from afar, give them a reason to come closer, and keep their attention for a while. If you have no other principle employed, contrast should be the one.

Beyond the obvious contrast of black and white, complementary color schemes can create a dramatic and often graphic sense of drama. Consider a highly charged red-and-green palette in a pattern. If you continually use the same dose of each complement, it can be jarring without any place to rest the eye. I like to build up to a contrast by supporting it with other medium values or less saturated colors. In other words, allow some colors to play a supporting role instead of the contrast duo stealing all the scenes. And then choose your moments to let a contrasting pair of colors bounce off each other here and there.

If you, however, are a "more is more" quilter and you have the habit of inviting every color you know to the party, then organizational contrast is your guest of honor.

The Open Borders Quilt (page 141) is the perfect example of using contrasting color pairs and contrast in light and dark to achieve a boldness that is not jarring. Every color is there, but there is no chaos. Or perhaps it is organized chaos. While there is black and white, they are never side by side. Rather they build toward each other in various values of many other colors.

CONSIDERING THE STORY

In summary, I will suggest that all of these elements and principles can be used *to tell a story*. While the elements and principles can be manipulated to convey meaning and emphasis, as we have learned, there are subtle emotion-triggering features at the artist's fingertips.

Art and craft history have recorded historical moments, given a face to the name of a fictional character we have only otherwise read about, and created scenes of joy or fear to motivate political movements. These various genres of art typically tell stories by setting figures before us as if in a theatrical presentation of the plot playing itself out in real or imagined life. There are, in fact, count-less historical quilts that feature narrative and historical moments through figurative shapes and objects that are awe-inspiring. Art does imitate, and even perpetuate, life.

As quilters, we can honor a place, person, or personal memory with our quilts. One could argue these goals are merely a way to entertain us and occupy our thoughts as we physically produce the work. While that is true, I am also learning that this recordkeeping of a life lived is meaningful to me. And someday maybe it will be mean-ingful to my family. Keep in mind it is completely accept-able for your personal narrative to be kept private and shared just with yourself. However, when you label the quilt, maybe you would find it appropriate to name your inspiration even in the simplest way. Future historians will be glad you did.

The Adjusting Her Crown Collage (page 175) tells a story of a poignant time in my life.

Patchwork School

When I first tiptoed into quilt making in 2005, I already had a fairly extensive history with sewing, mostly garment-making. Despite this level of comfort, so many aspects of quilt making, particularly the tools and the techniques, were entirely new to me. Over time, I have developed a deep reverence for many traditional methods of patchwork. I have packed my favorite methods into my bag of tricks—and into this chapter.

Beyond the unique tools and techniques, there is also the *language* of quilt making. The language of quilt blocks and their rich history is a book unto itself. There are, however, several block styles that I return to frequently as their features invite certain compositional opportunities in my quilt designing.

While I consider the blocks to be the building units for my quilts, I consider appliqué to be the flourishing "garden" that can make designs truly come alive. It is this combination of traditional patchwork and exploratory appliqué that has landed me in my quilting happy place.

No matter how deep or shallow your sewing or quilting experience may be, I'm happy to offer a concise head start on my methods. Whether this chapter serves as your first real primer, or as a simple refresher, my hope is that it will get you excited and confident to begin the quilt projects.

MATERIAL CHOICES

FABRIC

Patchwork disciplines across countless cultures reveal choices that were made for the sake of beauty and just as many choices made for the sake of sustainability. Very often patchwork was (and still is) a recycling of cloth items in order to extend a material's life and usefulness as a new object. In this reusing of materials, we have seen silk, denim, felt, velveteen, polyester, simple woven, textured woven, and countless more fabrics included in patchwork quilts.

All fabric types can be classified as synthetic, natural, or blended in their fiber content. I think of these main categories of fabric as the first consideration in making material choices. There are no rules about combining multiple types in one piece, and there are plenty of gorgeous historical quilts that prove that point. However, considering the final use of a piece and its required care may help you decide just how much freedom you're comfortable engaging.

Art quilts that are intended to only ever be on display on the wall of your home or submitted to quilt shows for viewing don't need the same amount of regular cleaning as functional quilts. You also might not care how soft it is, or how it drapes, or how warm the piece is as it is purely meant to be a visual feast. So if you can sew through it, *you can quilt with it.*

If you're making a quilt for a new baby there are different considerations. This is a quilt that might get thrown in the wash frequently along with the crib bedding. Simple cotton woven is a great choice because it is so easy to wash and dry. Not to mention the materials are breathable as well as hopefully nice and soft against baby's skin. I love using cotton lawn or voile for baby quilts.

Somewhere in the middle of only needing to be beautiful on the wall and exclusively needing to function for warmth is the type of quilt that is a little of both. Maybe this is the quilt that you have on display but folded at the end of your bed and not on the wall. The quilts that play this role in my house will get washed maybe only once a year or less. Therefore, I could use slightly more delicate fabrics.

A standard medium-weight "quilting cotton" has come to be used pervasively in the quilting world, and this is due to it being readily available and very user friendly. If you're new to quilting (or sewing), these cottons are a wonderful place to start, because the fabric behaves very uniformly in cutting, sewing, ironing, and washing.

Fine fabrics like lawns, voiles, and woven fabrics from India are among my favorites to work with mostly because of my love for needle-turn appliqué and hand quilting. These finer fabrics are so easy to sink your needle into, and the resulting quilts have the loveliest hand. If cuddle-ability is a rating, they score very high.

▶ *The fabrics you choose for your quilts are a very personal decision and one that reflects you as the quilt maker more than anything. We tend to grow and change in our preferences over time, and that evolution can include not only fabric type but also the print styles and colors that we choose to combine.*

BATTING CHOICES

I'll start at the end and share that long ago I found a favorite brand and type of quilt batting and I generally use it no matter what kind of quilt I am making (Quilter's Dream® Bamboo). I chose my favorite based on how easy it is to "needle" when I am hand quilting. If I spend a full day hand quilting through 100% cotton batting compared to this favorite blend, I find my hand gets more tired. The blend of bamboo, silk, Tencel™, and cotton lends itself to a softness and drape that is not overly "lofty" or thick. Even though I came to like it first for the hand-quilting performance, I still use it when I employ machine quilting because the thickness and warmth is perfect for my quilt style and climate. Let's go over a few notes on what to consider if you're still looking for your cozy, fluffy happy place with quilt batting.

LOFT

"Loft" as it relates to batting refers to how thick or fluffy a batting is, as well as the density of that thickness. The specific blend of Quilter's Dream® Bamboo is a relatively thin batting that has a very stable and dense quality to it. The loft of a batting can vary even within one fiber type. So you can have a very thin 100% cotton batting or a very thick one. The same is true for wool, polyester, recycled batting, or any blend of those fibers. The loft density and fiber type both affect the warmth of the quilt batting. One more note about loft is how it affects the look of your quilt stitches. If your batting has a very thin loft, the quilting stitches will not have a big impact on the texture of your quilt whether machine or hand quilted. However, if your batting is especially thick, the tight stitches that pull the quilt layers toward each other will result in a much more dimensional effect.

FIBER

I have already noted a few different types of fiber content in battings, and just like with fabrics you have natural, synthetic, and blended fibers to choose from. The variations in fiber content not only affect the warmth of the quilt but also influence the overall cost to make your quilt.

I am partial to natural fibers in my quilts mostly due to the breathability, my warmer climate, and the fact that I am also using natural fibers in my fabric choices. If you want a quilt to be extra warm, a wool batting can be a wonderful choice. Just keep in mind if you're using mostly dark-colored fabrics, there are darker-colored battings to choose from as well. Fibers from wool battings have a tendency to "beard" or float through the surface of the quilt. I learned this the hard way with a white wool batting sneaking through a dark navy fabric backing on my quilt!

QUILT-ABILITY

If you plan to hire a machine quilter, and you shared with the quilter your quilting style, it's a good idea to ask the quilter to suggest the right kind of batting for your project. Since I had a preference from the start, I sent a roll of my favorite batting to Melissa Kelley, who machine-quilted many quilts for this book. (She and her husband Patrick run Sew Shabby Quilting.)

Some batting is very stable (often with a "scrim" coating on the surface to hold all the fiber in place) and therefore you do not need to stitch it very densely. If you're performing the machine quilting yourself, you may appreciate a batting that is fusible so that ironing the quilt sandwich is all that is needed to "baste" the layers together.

It's good to start small if you're trying out a new batting (or quilter) for the first time. Maybe begin with a baby quilt, or even a quilted pillow sham.

THREADS

The most important considerations in thread for me are the quality and fiber content. Your time making a quilt should be rewarded with a quality thread, and the quilt will age better if the thread's fiber content matches the fabric's fiber content. I have seen a polyester thread essentially cut through cotton fabric over time because the polyester, being practically indestructible, becomes sharp against a gently softening cotton.

While there are multiple brands that offer quality, my favorite is Aurifil. The thread (like many) is mercerized, which is a process that provides strength and sheen. I use the 50wt for machine sewing, hand sewing, hand appliqué, and hand basting my quilts. (There is a finer 80wt that many use for appliqué, but staying with the 50wt has worked well for me.) I don't use it often, but there is also a slightly heavier 40wt that is a bit more durable. This would be nice for topstitching, machine embroidery, or machine quilting. Even more decorative in nature is the 12wt (and an even thicker 8wt), which I use for hand quilting. I also have a lot of experience with Anchor pearl cotton and the 8wt is nice for hand quilting. I do prefer the Aurifil as I find the texture does not wear down as I sew and there seems to be a bit more grip to hold knots well.

As for my color choices, I tend to reach for something somewhat neutral when sewing patchwork. And neutral to me doesn't just mean beige or gray, but also lavender or other "between" shades or pale colors. I mostly just try to avoid bright white, black, or highly saturated and pure colors.

Choosing just one color for the more decorative parts of your quilt such as the hand quilting or machine quilting always feels like a big decision. I often consider how it looks against the quilt back as much as I do the front. My favorite shades to hand quilt with are hot pink, saffron yellow, a warm cream, and a rich amber brown. I have never made a quilt that does not look good with one of these shades.

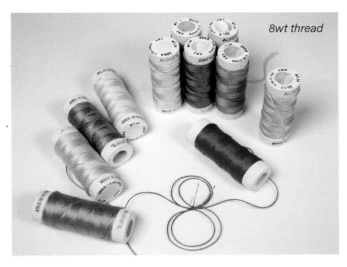

8wt thread

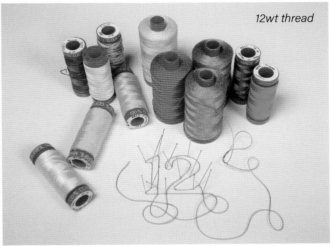

12wt thread

50wt thread

TOOLS OF THE TRADE

Certain tools in quilting only become obvious or necessary when embarking on a new technique, and there is naturally plenty of overlap with basic sewing tools. I will share my real-life must-haves and only mention brands when I think they are important. I have a tendency to take an overly simple approach to everything.

CUTTING

I find the quality and sharpness of cutting tools extremely important. Taking care of your scissors by only using them for the task they are intended for will extend their life and improve your experience. Here are my can't-live-without cutting tools and their primary role in my cutting.

LARGE FABRIC SHEARS

I was raised on large dressmaking shears because my first entry to cutting fabric was for making garments. I still keep a pair in my supplies because they are useful for cutting large pieces of fabric from a bolt, or even from a roll of batting. For simple cuts that are longer than your cutting mat (for instance, a full width of fabric) and do not need to be precise other than generally straight, these are perfect. I really like the weight of the classic Gingher scissors. If cared for, they will last a lifetime.

MEDIUM SCISSORS

The next size down in my cutting are those that I use for more precise shapes. The Karen Kay Buckley Perfect Scissors are my favorite, and they come in many sizes. They are lightweight, extra sharp, and I always get an accurate cut, which is especially important if I am cutting on a traced line for appliqué.

CRAFT SCISSORS

What I refer to as craft scissors are those that you can cut nonfabric materials with. It is best to have a designated pair for cutting any paper, pattern tissue, card stock, template plastic, tracing paper, and even your interfacings.

THREAD SNIPS

Snips come in various formations from beautiful embroidery scissors to extremely sharp and knifelike spring-loaded varieties. Just consider the application and whether you want a very sharp tip to the snips. I don't want a really sharp tip anywhere near any delicate handwork I am doing, so I typically use my small classic embroidery scissors (yes, the ones that look like a stork) when sewing on the couch.

SEAM RIPPER

I use a seam ripper for exactly what you might expect—mistakes. However, what I most likely use it for more than anything is to loosen and lift out the temporary machine basting on my appliqué shapes before I make the permanent needle-turn stitches.

▶ *My favorite cutting tools*

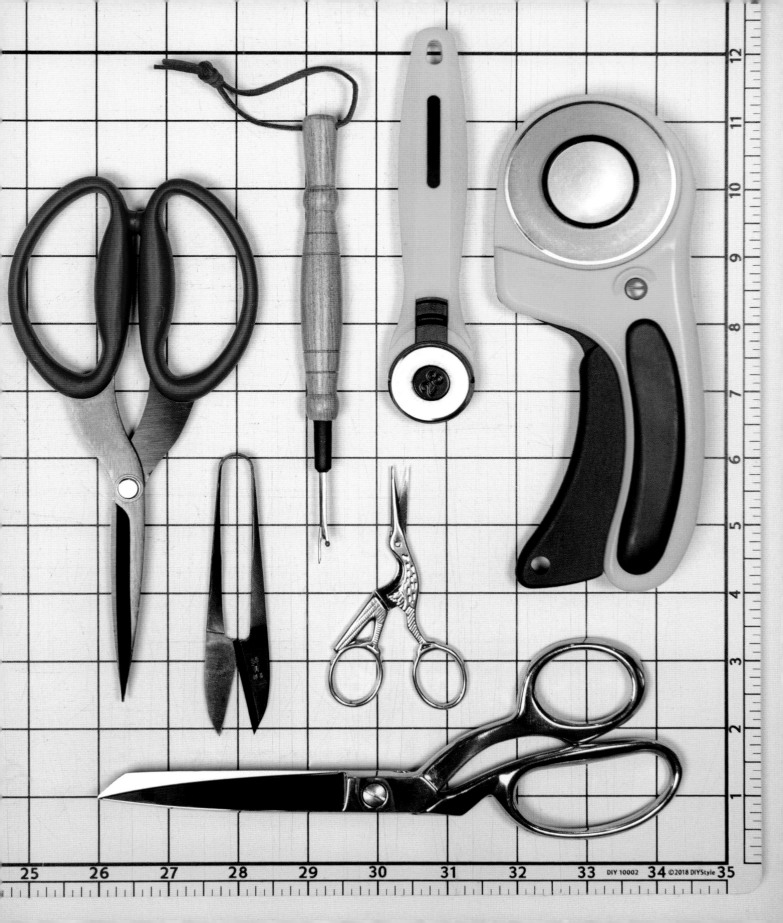

ROTARY CUTTER

As I have explained to my children (all seven of them at some point over the years), this is a pizza cutter for fabric. The accuracy and opportunity to cut through multiple fabric layers at once make them indispensable for patchwork cutting. I have not found a brand that I like more than the classic Olfa.

In conjunction with my cutting grids and cutting mat, I use the large or medium size (60 mm or 45 mm) for all straight line cutting when I am going through anywhere from one to six layers of fabric (sometimes eight layers with a fresh blade). I use a small 28 mm size in conjunction with my acrylic template shapes and a mat when I am cutting any pieces that are smaller or curved.

CUTTING MATS

You cannot use a rotary cutter without having the companion self-healing mat underneath. These mats come in all sizes printed with various measurement markings. Three different sizes are indispensable to me.

The large 24" × 36" (61 × 91.4 cm) size is imperative for my cutting table, and I have two side by side. The markings help me measure and cut all basic shapes, and even bias angles. The 24" (61 cm) is tall enough to cut standard cotton folded off the bolt, and the length of 36" (91.4 cm) is helpful in measuring out longer pieces. I often use the straight edge of the mat to run my fabric shears against when making a simple cut from a bolt.

The other two sizes I like are a smallish rectangle (12" × 18" [30.5 × 45.7 cm]) and a small circle (18" [45.7 cm]) that sits on a turning lazy Susan wheel. I like the portability of the small rectangle and sometimes keep it next to me at the machine for small cutting between seam work steps. I also take it into the house for light cutting if I am working with a movie on. The rotating circular mat allows me to turn smaller, fussier pieces without lifting the piece or repositioning the angle of my hand or my body to cut all sides of the piece.

MEASURING TOOLS

Unless you're a completely improvisational quilter, you will need to measure all of your cuts. The cutting mats provide measurement markings, but you'll need to use a clear cutting grid in conjunction with the mat to cut your desired piece sizes.

ACRYLIC CUTTING GRIDS

In addition to being a general-purpose measuring device, cutting grids provide a straight edge to cut along with the rotary cutter. The clear material and regular measurement markings allow you to see through to your fabric and position any desired fabric design elements more accurately.

Rectangles

I use a few different types that are all 24" (61 cm) long because they encompass a 44" (111.8 cm) width of fabric folded on center.

3½" × 24" (8.9 × 61 cm)—for quick cutting off a bolt and for cutting narrow strips

8½" × 24" (21.6 × 61 cm)—for all-purpose cutting off a bolt, smaller pieces and borders

6" × 24" (15.2 × 61 cm)—I use this one as I do the others, but I also use this size like a cardboard fabric bolt to wrap sizable fabric pieces around. I then slip out the cutting grid and fold the fabric over once more before storing. This keeps all my stacks of larger yardage tidy and the same size on my shelves.

Squares

Most of the time I am using square grids to trim or "square" blocks to prepare for assembly; for that reason I prefer them to have the ½" (13 mm) increment beyond the block size. My favorite sizes are related to the block sizes I tend to create most in my quilts: 6½" (16.5 cm), 9½" (24.1 cm), 12½" (31.8 cm), and 16½" (41.9 cm).

Assorted Shape Rulers

Suffice it to say if it is a geometric shape, there is an acrylic ruler for it. Everything from diamonds and hexagons to octagons and triangles in every degree are available to help you with traditional and contemporary quilt blocks alike, and in every size.

I continually use organically shaped acrylic and Mylar shapes for appliqué cutting. This is partly because I manufacture them to use with my quilt patterns. The corresponding acrylic and Mylar shapes work together for marking and/or cutting the fabric shape and for preparing to crease the seam allowance for needle-turn or raw-edge appliqué. Appliqué Adventures (page 54) will detail their use more specifically.

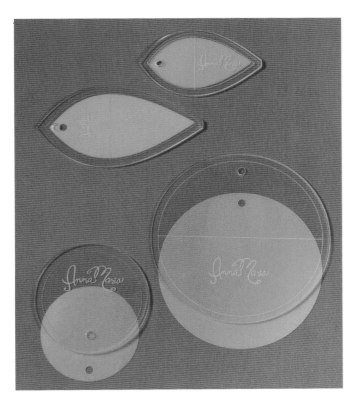

A few of the acrylic and mylar templates I manufacture for use with my quilt patterns

MARKING TOOLS

Before we dive into drawing on fabric, I cannot express enough how helpful it is to have graph paper on hand in your sewing space. Even if you do not explicitly design your own quilts, it is wonderful for sketching plans as you think through a pattern, or any amendments you might make to it. Recreating the general layout of a pattern you're following and making a fabric or color plan with notes or even colored pencils is a wonderful way to warm up to starting a quilt.

With basic patchwork, I tend to cut and sew a shape and never mark it. The need for marking tools is really defined by what kind of quilting techniques you do the most. I primarily do pretty straightforward patchwork, plenty of appliqué, and also hand quilting. I therefore use marking tools that suit those general tasks.

If I'm marking something in patchwork, it might be a "start" or "stop" line for a specific technique like performing a Y-seam, and for this I would use a simple No. 2 pencil (Ticonderoga is my favorite). If it will not be hidden by the seam allowance, I use a chalk pencil that can be brushed or washed away. I do not recommend "disappearing" ink (either by air, water, or heat) as I continue to hear varying reviews on the disappearing success. I simply do my best to make marks in a way that will be hidden.

For tracing appliqué shapes onto fabric (please make sure you're sitting down), I honestly will use just a No. 2 pencil or even a fine-line ink pen or ballpoint pen as folding the edge in my needle-turn process will hide it. I specifically do not want an ink pen that disappears with the heat of the iron, because I may or may not press the shapes before they are completely sewn.

My favorite tool for marking hand-quilting lines is the Hera™ Marker by Clover. This comfortable-to-hold plastic tool has a sharp (not razor) curved edge that you can press into the fabric and glide in your desired direction, and it creates a visible crease in the fabric. This temporary crease is almost always visible enough to see in good lighting, so stitching along the line is simple.

NEEDLES, PINS & THIMBLES

NEEDLES

If I were to only ever buy one set of needles, it would be an assorted-size pack of embroidery needles. This gives me the sharpness, various lengths, and eye sizes that I like to use for hand sewing, appliqué, and hand quilting. But please do experiment to your heart's content.

A classic appliqué needle is very small and short; however, because I load multiple stitches at once, I prefer a longer, more general sewing needle or "sharps" in various sizes. The same would be true when completing the hand-sewing finish on my binding. Because I also often want a needle with a larger eye to accommodate the thickness of the Aurifil 12wt for hand quilting, I always have multiple sizes of embroidery needles on hand.

PINS

Quilting pins: Since I grew up making garments, I was accustomed to the standard smallish straight pin, which is just fine for quilting. However, I really like the longer quilting pins with the larger heads because I like the ability to feel and know where they are as I look away from my work from time to time.

Safety pins: I don't do much machine quilting; however, when I do, it is helpful to have curved safety pins to baste the quilt layers together. The curve saves your wrist when pinning dozens into the quilt layers compared with a traditional straight safety pin.

Awl / stiletto: Maybe less obvious for your quilting but really helpful, the long narrow tips of these tools allow you to use something other than your finger to hold a small fold or layer of fabric in place as it is just about to pass under the sewing machine needle. In addition to saving your finger from an accident, it can provide a more accurate hold when you're focused on precision.

THIMBLES

When I am hand quilting, pushing the needle through thick layers for hours on end can take a toll on whatever fingertip you use to push the needle through. Or the opposite nonworking hand that receives the needle or feels the motion from underneath could get a prick here and there.

While all the details of how or where you need a thimble vary depending on your technique, I personally have never gotten comfortable with any sort. So, I encourage you to experiment. I have settled on a bandage on my middle right finger because that is the fingertip that pushes the needle through. I like the bandage because I can still feel where the needle is, but it doesn't hurt.

▶ *Some of my must-have tools: pins, needles, an awl, and bandages!*

SEWING MACHINE

I have sewn exclusively on Janome sewing machines for more than twenty years and have never been disappointed by the stitch quality or the durability. No matter what brand or model you have, the following features are those that get the most action in my quilting.

Straight stitch: Quite obviously the machine needs this basic stitch, but you'll want to vary the length of the stitch for various processes like piecework, binding, temporary basting, and more.

¼" (0.6 cm) foot attachment & plate markings: A built-in system of easily aligning the edge of your fabric in a way that achieves accurate seam allowances as you sew is imperative. I personally can take or leave the ¼" (0.6 cm) foot (probably due to my garment-making history), but I am mentioning it because I know most quilters love using it.

Appliqué stitch: It may or may not be important for you to have anything more than a zigzag stitch, but if you want to explore decorative stitches for appliqué, more than the basics can be delightful. I never would have found my favorite little cross-stitch-like style that I use on my machine appliqué if my Janome had not had so many choices to encourage my experimenting.

Presser foot adjustment: Every sewing machine will allow you to adjust the tension of the thread and therefore stitch, but adjusting the pressure or the presser foot against the fabric passing underneath is of great benefit.

Free motion capable: The machine's mechanism that moves or "feeds" the fabric under the needle is called the feed dogs. However, if you want to freely move the fabric around for free-motion quilting, you might like to give those dogs a rest. In this instance, you'll need to have the option to "drop" the feed dogs so you can move the quilt sandwich around in any curvy or pictorial direction you would like.

Extension table & "right of needle" space: If curvy quilting sounds like you, it is really helpful to have a sewing machine with the option to expose the free-arm and attach an extension table. This extra space is helpful for keeping your quilt in progress supported across a larger area. Additionally, the bulk management of machine quilting can be greatly helped if your sewing machine has a lot of space between the needle and the controls area to the right.

IRONS & PRESSING SURFACE

Ironing board: My ironing board is nothing special or expensive. I use a basic, but quality, home ironing board, and there are larger, heftier versions available for you to try.

Pressing mat: I have created a very long, thick ironing mat (plenty of how-to instructions out there to make your own) that I place on my work counter for larger items, and it is very useful. If you have a small space, you might prefer a tabletop pressing mat that is more portable and less awkward than a folding ironing board.

Iron: One thing is certain, you will press every seam and fabric that you touch in your quilt, so the iron is not to be overlooked. While there are, of course, irons with every bell and whistle on the market, a quality iron that has steam, but also the option for *no steam*, is really all you need. I currently use an Oliso iron.

ADHESIVES

The list of available glues, interfacings, papers, and fusible interfacing is infinite, so I am going to stick to those that I use in the projects contained in this book. Each of these will be elaborated in Appliqué Adventures (page 54). Because of the permanence of this material, it is ideal to use even when creating art using cut fabric collage techniques.

Glue stick: I love the Sewline brand of glue sticks because the glue is supple, reliable, and easy to reposition whether it is fresh or dry. I use this for temporary placement of my appliqué pieces before I sew them in place either by hand or at the machine.

Pellon® 805 Wonder-Under®: This is a sheer, single layer glue sheet that has a temporary paper backing. I use this under the heat of an iron to glue appliqué pieces to the background before machine sewing them down. This is a permanent glue once pressed with heat.

BUILDING BLOCKS

Welcome to the quilt construction site, no hard hat required! In this section, I am offering tutorials on some tried-and-true and, mostly, very traditional quilt blocks. All of these blocks are used in the quilts throughout the book and you can refer back to these tutorials when you're called upon to include them in a project. One quilt project might ask for a 3" (7.6 cm) Half-Square Triangle and another might ask for one that is 12" (30.5 cm). No matter the cut and finished size required, the assembly techniques offered here remain the same unless otherwise noted in specific pattern instructions.

We will begin with the simplest block and work our way up to more advanced blocks. But first, a few notes:

1. Assume patchwork is right sides together and ¼" (6 mm) seam allowances unless otherwise noted.

2. When a block size is offered in the projects it will be the "finished size," which means its size after it is assembled into a quilt. So a "9" (22.9 cm) block" means a 9½" (24.1 cm) block before it's finished.

3. "Squaring" blocks will always mean to trim them to a size that is ½" (13 mm) bigger than the finished size.

4. The fabric requirements in the quilt patterns will reflect the palette that is in the feature quilt. Changing colors, repeat styles, and fussy cutting will affect your requirements.

5. The cutting for blocks will be instructed either by noting the piece size dimensions or by directing you to a specific template at the back of the book.

HALF-SQUARE TRIANGLE (HST)

This lovely two-patch block is a simple square that is divided on an angle by a seam between two fabrics. While you can cut two different right triangles and sew them together, the following method yields two HSTs at a time. It is the perfect method when you aren't fussy about fabric placement. The angled seam and final squaring will eat up more than the standard ¼" (6 mm) seam allowance, so the cut size is generally ⅞" (2.2 cm) or larger than the desired finished size.

1. Cut a same-sized square from two different fabrics *(Fig. 1)*.

2. Lay the pair of fabrics right sides together with all edges aligned.

3. From one corner to the opposite, use a pencil and straight edge to draw a straight line across at a 45-degree angle on the wrong side. Pin squares together at center.

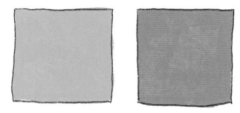

Fig. 1

Anna Maria's Blueprint Quilting

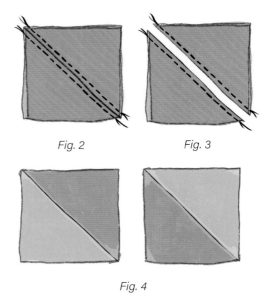

Fig. 2   Fig. 3

Fig. 4

4.   Sew ¼" (6 mm) to the right of the drawn line from one corner to the other. Now repeat on the other side of the line ¼" (6 mm) away from the drawn line again (Fig. 2).

5.   Carefully cut on the drawn line (Fig. 3). Open each block to its right side. Press from both sides, and press seam allowances as desired.

6.   Square both HST Blocks so that the seam is ending exactly in the opposite corners and dimensions are the desired finished size plus seam allowance. For example, for a finished 5" (12.5 cm) block, trim to 5½" (14 cm) (Fig. 4).

QUARTER-SQUARE TRIANGLE (QST)

This smart four-patch block with an hourglass look is a bit of an older sister to the HST. Once two HSTs are created, we go another few steps to end with two QSTs. The starting size for the squares will be healthier than that of the HST as you will make an additional seam. Generally, you will begin with a cut size that is 1¼" (3.2 cm) bigger than the desired finished size.

1.   Follow steps 1 through 5 from the HST instructions to finish with two HSTs (don't trim).

2.   Place the two HSTs right sides together, with their seams aligned, but also so that opposite fabrics are laying against each other. This will ensure that you achieve the "hourglass" design in your final Quarter-Square Triangles.

3.   Repeat the drawing step of the HST, but in a way that crosses over the seam at a perpendicular angle.

4.   Now repeat the sewing steps of the HST ¼" (6 mm) to either side from the line drawn in the previous step (Fig. 5).

5.   Carefully cut on the drawn line (Fig. 6). Open each block to its right side. Press from both sides, and press seam allowances as desired.

6.   Square both QST Blocks so that all four seams end in four corners and dimensions are the desired finished size plus ½" (13 mm) (Fig. 7).

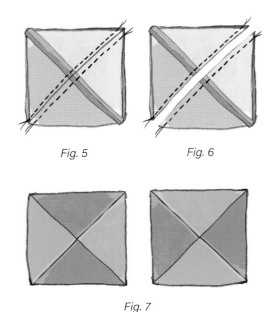

Fig. 5   Fig. 6

Fig. 7

STRIP PIECED BLOCK

A Strip Pieced Block is exactly what it sounds like. You're essentially building stripes with fabric. The following tutorial will create a simple three-patch block that ends in a square. These dimensions can be endlessly manipulated, both in terms of the finished block size and in terms of the width of the stripes. The following block finishes at 9" (22.9 cm).

1. Cut two strips of one fabric from selvage to selvage that are 3½" (8.9 cm) wide.

2. Cut a third strip of fabric from a second fabric that is also 3½" (8.9 cm) wide.

3. Sew the strips one to the next on their long edges, but alternating the fabrics. This will result in the matching strips being on the outside edges of the center strip of a different color.

4. Press the seam allowances all in the same direction.

5. Use a cutting grid to trim off the first uneven selvage ends for a clean edge. From that edge measure and "sub-cut" off a 9½" (24.1 cm) section of the strip piecing (Fig. 8). (Sub-cut simply means you will make a more specific cut, after making general cuts or preparatory sewing.)

6. Continue to sub-cut 9½" (24.1 cm) sections (you should be able to cut four sections from standard 44" to 45" (111.8 to 114.3 cm)-wide fabric).

You now have four blocks that would make an interesting woven effect if you alternated their directions for assembly.

9-PATCH BLOCK

While you can create any number of squares in a checkerboard-style block, a square block will be the same number of squares high as it is wide. The two-color 9-Patch Block is a very classic variety and the base structure for countless variations. You can create these with nine individually cut squares of the same size, but the following method takes the strip-piecing process through a few more steps to increase efficiency for making several 9-Patch Blocks from the same two colors. The following block finishes at 9" (22.9 cm).

1. Follow steps 1 through 4 of the Strip Pieced Block.

2. Repeat steps 1 through 4 of the Strip Pieced Block but this time alternate the fabric colors the opposite way when sewing them. So, if the section you end with after step 4 is red/pink/red, make sure the next section is pink/red/pink.

3. After trimming the first clean edge of each section, sub-cut both color varieties of strip piecing into 3½" (8.9 cm) widths so the resulting pieces are 3½" × 9½" (8.9 × 24.1 cm) (Fig. 9). Continue until you have cut as many pieces as possible from both color strip varieties (or the number you want).

4. Now sew three of these pieces together, using an alternate color in the center of two same colors to create the checkerboard effect (Fig. 10). It is helpful to "nest" the seam allowances so that they are going the opposite direction at seam allowance intersections.

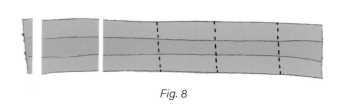

Fig. 8

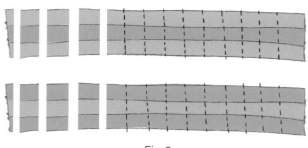

Fig. 9

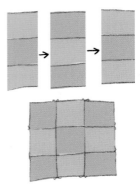

Fig. 10

It's good to note that any two-color checkerboard-style block that is a square and has an odd number of patches will require you to make two different colors (arrangements) of strip piecing to achieve the effect. So the same is true for a 25-patch block.

16-PATCH BLOCK

The next step in quilt math after a block that is 3 by 3 patches is 4 by 4, and it is actually even simpler. The following block finishes at 12" (30.5 cm). See the Basket of Flowers Quilt (page 135) for an example of 16-Patch Blocks.

1. Follow steps 1 through 4 of the Strip Pieced Block except:

    - Cut two strips of each color for a total of four.

    - Sew all four strips together alternating color and ending with a 12½" × width of fabric (WOF) (31.8 cm × WOF) piece.

2. Sub-cut 3½" (8.9 cm) pieces from this section.

3. To assemble four together in a checkerboard layout, you will only need to spin every other piece upside down.

Any two-color checkerboard-style block that is square and has an even number of patches will allow you to only create one style of strip piecing, and simply alternate the orientation in assembly.

CUSTOM-BUILT CHECKERBOARD

Now that you have the logic of how this style of block works, you can really play with the outcome by increasing the number of colors, the number and size of patches, and the overall size. You can still create uniformity and variety all in one block by reusing strip piecing in more than one place so the block is still balanced in color.

The patchwork triangles that edge the Open Borders Quilt (page 141) are assembled from individual squares; however, they are all uniform in fabric placement to create a pattern around the border.

SNOWBALL BLOCK

The Snowball Block can be thought of as a square that has had a little work done on its corners. Though it is all straight lines, from a distance, when many of these blocks are sewn adjacent to each other, they look a bit roundish, like a snowball. The following block will finish at 9" (22.9 cm).

1. Cut one 9½" (24.1 cm) square from one color, and cut four 3½" (8.9 cm) squares from a second color.

2. On the wrong side of the small squares, draw an angled line from one corner to the other.

3. Lay one small square onto any corner of the large square so that both edges are aligned. Also make sure that the drawn line is not pointing to the corner, but to the perpendicular edges.

4. Sew on the drawn line before trimming off the excess ¼" (6 mm) away from the seam *(Fig. 11)*.

5. Open the small triangle to reveal the new corner, and press well.

6. Repeat steps 3 through 5 on the remaining three corners to complete the Snowball Block *(Fig. 12)*.

SHOOFLY BLOCK

To create the Shoofly Block, we are going to combine the 9-Patch and the Snowball into one block. Technically this would still be considered a 9-Patch. However, the corner patches are actually HSTs. Like everything in quilt making there are a couple of ways that you can go about this. Let's do it the obvious way. The following block will finish at 9" (22.9 cm).

1. Follow steps 1 through 4 of the 9-Patch Block to complete a block.

2. Cut four 3½" (8.9 cm) squares in the third color.

3. Follow steps 2 through 6 of the Snowball Block to complete the Shoofly Block *(Fig. 13)*.

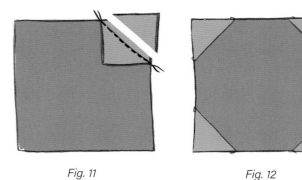

Fig. 11   Fig. 12

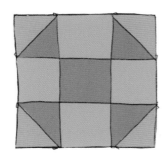

Fig. 13

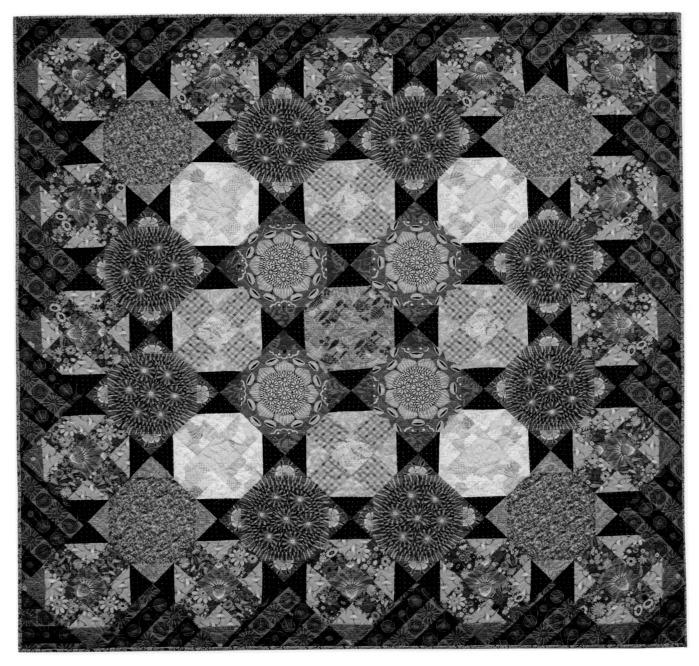

Snowball and Shoofly Blocks are set on point for added interest in the Kaleidoscope Quilt (page 129).

LOG CABIN BLOCK

As someone who was utterly obsessed with Lincoln Logs as a kid, this block had me at "log cabin." Rounds of rectangles are sewn around a center square and you can create *sew* much variety and interest by changing the color, value, and size of the pieces. Seam accuracy is your friend when building these cabins; being a little off with this many seams can result in more than a little off once complete. Take your time. The following block will finish at 12" (30.5 cm), and it is up to you how you'd like to arrange color.

The following pieces each have a letter order in the block map; label them if you wish as you cut. Also keep in mind that all of the strips below are the same width so you can cut strips from a full width of fabric first before sub-cutting them in the lengths detailed below.

1. Cut a square that is 3½" (8.9 cm). This is piece A.

2. Cut the first round of rectangles from your desired fabrics in the following sizes:
   - B: 2" × 3½" (5.1 × 8.9 cm) (cut one)
   - C and D: 2" × 5" (5.1 × 12.7 cm) (cut two)
   - E: 2" × 6½" (5.1 × 16.5 cm) (cut one)

3. Cut the second round of rectangles from your desired fabrics in the following sizes:
   - F: 2" × 6½" (5.1 × 16.5 cm) (cut one)
   - G and H: 2" × 8" (5.1 × 20.3 cm) (cut two)
   - I: 2" × 9½" (5.1 × 24.1 cm) (cut one)

4. Cut the third round of rectangles from your desired fabrics in the following sizes:
   - J: 2" × 9½" (5.1 × 24.1 cm) (cut one)
   - K and L: 2" × 11" (5.1 × 27.9 cm) (cut two)
   - M: 2" × 12½" (5.1 × 31.8 cm) (cut one)

5. Begin by sewing A to B. Open and press seam allowances toward B.

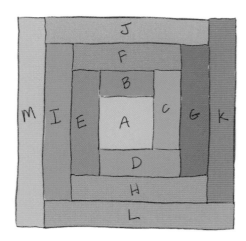

Fig. 14

6. Sew C to the right edge of the unit. Open and press seam allowances toward C.

7. Sew D to the lower edge of the unit. Open and press seam allowances toward D.

8. Sew E to the left edge of the unit. Open and press seam allowances toward E. This is round one.

9. Repeat steps 5 through 8, sewing pieces F, G, H, and I to the unit made so far. This is round two.

10. Repeat steps 5 through 8 with pieces J, K, L, and M to the unit made so far. This is round three. Press the final block well *(Fig. 14)*.

QUARTER LOG CABIN BLOCK

Think of this log cabin as the guest quarters. It carries the same features and look of the original cabin, but we are only building on two sides of the "center" (which will actually be a corner when we are done). While you can certainly arrive at this look by taking one finished Log Cabin Block and slicing it into four pieces, this method ensures your seams land where you want them. The following block finishes at 9" (22.9 cm) and alternates between two values.

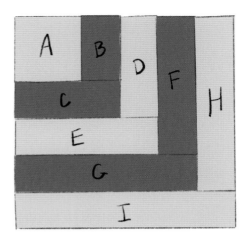

Fig. 15

The following pieces each have a letter order in the block map; label them if you wish as you cut.

1. Cut one square that is 3½" (8.9 cm) from a light-colored fabric (A).

2. From a dark-colored fabric, cut rectangles that are 2" × 3½" (5.1 × 8.9 cm) (B) and 2" × 5" (5.1 × 12.7 cm) (C).

3. From a light-colored fabric, cut rectangles that are 2" × 5" (5.1 × 12.7 cm) (D) and 2" × 6½" (5.1 × 16.5 cm) (E).

4. From a dark-colored fabric, cut rectangles that are 2" × 6½" (5.1 × 16.5 cm) (F) and 2" × 8" (5.1 × 20.3 cm) (G).

5. From a dark-colored fabric, cut rectangles that are 2" × 8" (5.1 × 20.3 cm) (H) and 2" × 9½" (5.1 × 24.1 cm) (I).

6. Sew B to the right-hand side of A. Press seam allowances toward B.

7. Sew C to the bottom side of the unit. Press seam allowances toward C.

8. Sew D to the right-hand side of the unit. Press seam allowances toward D.

9. Sew E to the bottom side of the unit. Press seam allowances toward E.

10. Sew F to the right-hand side of the unit. Press seam allowances toward F.

11. Sew G to the bottom side of the unit. Press seam allowances toward G.

12. Sew H to the right-hand side of the unit. Press seam allowances toward H.

13. Sew I to the bottom side of the unit. Press seam allowances toward I. Press entire block well *(Fig. 15)*.

WHIPPERSNAPPER BLOCK

I drafted this block several years ago and really like how foolproof the foundation piecing method is and I love the opportunity to use scraps. I named it "Whippersnapper" because combining several of these together can have very different visual effects depending on how you whip them around, and they come together in a snap. The following version will finish at 12" (30.5 cm). You will also want to have some tissue paper on hand for this foundation paper method.

1. Cut one square from dark fabric that is 13½" (34.3 cm).

2. Sub-cut the square on both angles so that you end with four triangles and set aside.

3. Cut multiple strips from medium-value scraps that vary in width from 1" (2.5 cm) to 2½" (6.4 cm). It is okay if some of them are short and some are long.

4. Cut multiple strips from lighter-value strips that have the same variation in width, but make sure that some are at least 18" (45.7 cm) or so long.

5. Use a 12½" (31.8 cm) square cutting grid to trace a square onto the tissue paper with a pencil.

(continued)

6. Then use a longer straight edge to draw the following lines inside the square:

   - A line one corner to the opposite
   - A line that is parallel to the angled line, but ¼" (6 mm) to one side
   - Another line that is parallel to the first, but ¼" (6 mm) to the other side
   - Repeat the above three lines but from the other pair of opposite corners *(Fig. 16)*

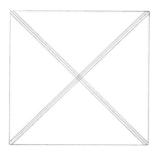

Fig. 16

7. Lay one of the dark triangles (right side facing up) into a triangular space created by the drawn lines, and align the top point with the highest set of lines (thereby hiding all the lines of that triangle). Pin the triangle in the few places in the center to keep in place.

8. Next lay a medium-value strip (wrong side up) over the angled line on the right-hand side of the triangle as shown in the illustration *(Fig. 17)*. Make sure the short end of the strip meets the farthest line to the left of the three lines going into the upper right-hand corner.

Fig. 17

9. Pin these layers in a few spots if desired before sewing (yes, through the paper, too) the outer edge with a ¼" (6 mm) seam allowance from the point of the triangle to the outer edge.

10. Turn the strip back to reveal the right side, finger press the seam nice and flat, and trim off any amount of the strip that is in excess of the square edge.

11. Repeat steps 8 through 10 in the same manner to build out the triangle with a variety of strips and you will notice they get smaller. Continue until the triangle is covered. It is okay for the outer edge to be irregular for now, but you will want to keep the center line even as you place strips.

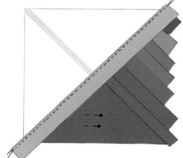

Fig. 18

12. You can give the strips a light pressing; just be sure you don't overly heat or steam the tissue to alter it in any way.

13. Now lay a light-tone strip (wrong side up) across the entire patchwork edge, so from one corner of the square to the other *(Fig. 18)*.

14. Sew this edge in place with a ¼" (6 mm) seam allowance; open to the right side and finger press. Continue this until the entire space is covered to the corner. Again, it is fine for the outer edges to be irregular, but all strips have to go beyond the outer lines.

15. Press the block well on the fabric side, then use the 12½" (31.8 cm) cutting grid to trim the block to a perfect square *(Fig. 19)*. Make sure the center angled lines are passing straight through the corners.

16. You can now lift the paper off of the back (it will come apart at the seams) and discard.

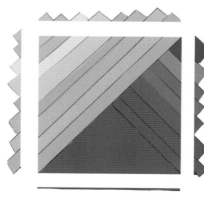

Fig. 19

Anna Maria's Blueprint Quilting

In the Basket of Flowers Quilt (page 135) the darkest fabric is the triangle, the medium fabrics are the small strips, and the lightest fabrics are the long strips.

LIGHT RAY BLOCK

When I first drafted this block, I searched and searched to find a traditional version, but the closest thing I could find was a sun block. While the four-piece ray formation is the same, mine only has the rays and no sun. Alas, I have always found it important to call a block by its common name in my quilts because I like continuing the history and hopefully encouraging quilters to get curious about that history too. All that said, you'll need to use the Light Ray templates (pages 188–189) for this one. The following version will finish at 12" (30.5 cm).

1. Choose four different fabrics for the four rays of your block and decide which position you want for each. Choose the two fabrics that you want to occupy the A and A-reverse position as noted on the block map and place them wrong sides together. Make sure the right side of what you want to be the A piece is facing up (Fig. 20).

2. Lay the A template (right side up) onto the pair of fabrics and cut two at the same time. Opening these fabrics to reveal the right side will also reveal the mirror image shape they bear.

3. Now lay the B template onto the pair of the fabrics that you would like to occupy the B and B-reverse positions as noted in the block map and cut. Make sure the right side of what you want to be the B piece is facing up. Use the template to cut both pieces at the same time.

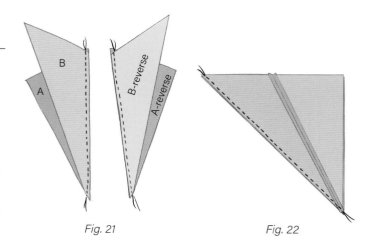

Fig. 21   *Fig. 22*

4. Sew the A piece to the B piece as shown (*Fig. 21*). Press seam allowances as desired.

5. Sew the B-reverse piece to the A-reverse piece in the same manner and press (*Fig. 21*).

6. Now sew the two units together on the long edge between B and B-reverse (*Fig. 22*).

7. Press seam allowance as desired to finish block.

GRANDMOTHER'S FAN BLOCK

Often simply called the Fan Block, this is another charmer that looks like its name. I simply adore this block, and you might have noticed that I am sneaking in the first real curve here (and not the optical illusion sort like the Snowball Block). I think this is a nice first entry to curves, and I will share the Fan Block as an appliqué onto a square foundation. When it comes time to sew a Fan Block in this book's projects, you're welcome to create one from a pieced method if you prefer. The following block uses the Small Fan template (page 186) and will finish at 9" (22.9 cm).

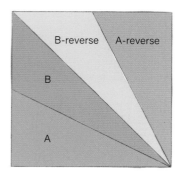

Fig. 20

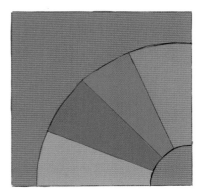

Fig. 23

1. Cut a square that measures 9½" (24.1 cm) from your background fabric.

2. Cut four different fan "blades" using the template from desired fabrics.

3. Sew one blade to the next until all four are assembled and press in one direction.

4. Layer the assembled "fan" over the square aligning side edges and pin or glue tack in place to prepare for appliqué.

5. Appliqué the fan as desired at the outer and inner edge. Choose from a few different techniques in Appliqué Adventures (page 54) *(Fig. 23)*.

Note that the inner corner can be covered with another shape and therefore you would not have to finish the edge. For example, in the Terrace Views Quilt (page 113) I place two of these blocks side by side so that they create a fully open fan or half circle. I also appliquéd a circle over the inner corners that meet between two blocks, to hide the unfinished edges of the fan blades.

DRESDEN PLATE (POINTED)

Scan to watch a tutorial.

If I had to choose a favorite quilt block, I might be partial to the Dresden Plate. The pointy blades that come together to make an interesting edge are so much easier to create than they appear. There are countless varieties of this block that have more or fewer blades and longer or shorter blades in one circle. You can sew this to a square background or let it float over any patchwork. The Dresden template (page 187) has a few different lengths to choose from which will vary the overall size. You can also choose any circular template for the center.

1. Use the Dresden template (cut with any of the length lines) to cut twenty blades from assorted fabrics.

2. Cut a circle from your desired Dresden center fabric.

3. Fold one blade right sides against itself on the vertical center as shown. Sew across the short folded top edge using a ¼" (6 mm) seam allowance *(Fig. 24)*. (You can continue more by chain piecing.)

4. Carefully trim the folded corner seam allowance at an angle, and open the vertical fold to make the blade flat, which will create a point at the top *(Fig. 25)*. Finger press the seam allowance open before flipping the point right side out. Press the point well, keeping the seam in the vertical center of the blade.

5. Repeat steps 3 and 4 for the remaining blade pieces to finish with twenty prepped blades.

(continued)

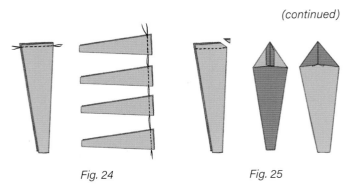

Fig. 24   *Fig. 25*

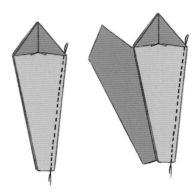

Fig. 26

6. Create a layout that you're happy with and begin sewing one to the next along their long edges and press in one direction or open *(Fig. 26)*. Pay careful attention to the accuracy of the ¼" (6 mm) seam allowance from one end to the other, and you might choose to backstitch at the beginning and end of each seam to secure.

7. Continue step 6 until you have joined five of the "blades" together. This is a fourth of the total circle and if accurately sewn it should be a right angle on the outer two straight edges. Set aside.

8. Repeat steps 6 and 7 until you have four units of the circle.

9. Join two of the units to create a half circle; press as desired. Repeat with the remaining two units. *(Fig. 27)*

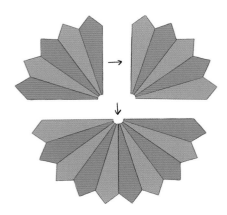

Fig. 27

10. Now join the two halves to create a whole Dresden Plate Block and press well. If the block does not lay flat, adjust the depth of one or more seams until it does.

11. This finished section can have a circle appliquéd in place at the center of the blades before you appliqué the Dresden onto a background. See Needle-Turn Appliqué (page 55) for instructions.

DRESDEN FAN VARIATIONS (QUARTER AND HALF)

Once you have seen how much fun Dresdens can be, you can really play around with the number of blades you include to create a whole variety of flower heads for your quilts. The resulting blocks look more like fans than plates. Here are a couple of simple ideas for you.

To make a Quarter Dresden Fan, follow the Dresden Plate instructions, but only cut 5 blades and only follow the instructions to step 7. This quarter fan can be sewn to the corner of a block, or it can be appliquéd to any background. Just be sure to turn and press long unfinished edges under before sewing by hand or machine.

To make a Half Dresden Fan, follow the Dresden Plate instructions, but only cut 10 blades and only follow the instructions to step 7. Instead of Step 8, only continue for another two units. Finish the Half Dresden Fan by completing step 9. The unfinished edge of this half fan can be sewn into a patchwork seam, or it can be appliquéd to any background. Just be sure to turn and press long unfinished edges under before sewing by hand or machine.

For both the Quarter and Half Dresden Fan you can still appliqué a circular (or oval) shape over the narrow ends of the fans, but you will wait to do this until after you have appliquéd the fan on its background. See the appliqué instructions in Appliqué Adventures (page 54) for some tips.

Anna Maria's Blueprint Quilting

DRESDEN PLATE (PETALS)

Fig. 28

The petal-edge variety does not have the opportunity to begin the Dresden Plate with a finished edge like the pointed variety, but the curved petals are very charming. The following steps are adapted only somewhat to create an alternating petal version of the block with fewer blades. Use the petal template and your choice of a circle template (pages 182–183) for cutting.

1. Cut one circle from your desired center fabric.

2. Cut six petal blades from one fabric and six petal blades from a second fabric.

3. As you did in the original Dresden Plate (Pointed) assembly (page 51), sew one petal to the next alternating fabrics. This seam will begin where the petal goes from being straight to curving. If it helps, you can mark this on your cut petals. This seam ends at the narrow end just like the original Dresden. Continue to join until you have assembled a set of three. Press seam allowances open.

4. Repeat step 3 but alternate the fabric the other way. You should now have two units that alternate the colors in different ways.

5. Repeat steps 3 and 4 for a total of four units.

6. Lay out the full circle to establish the every-other-color order between your four units. Sew two oppositely colored units to one another to create half of the circle.

7. Sew the remaining two units together in the same way.

8. Now sew the two halves together to create the full petal circle. Press all seam allowances open.

9. This finished section can have a circle appliquéd in place at the center of the block before you appliqué the block onto a background (*Fig. 28*). More notes on appliqué for the center and the petal edges are in the next section of the chapter.

APPLIQUÉ ADVENTURES

MATERIALS

I use most of the same fabrics for appliqué as I would for patchwork, except for very heavy fabrics like velveteen or for fabrics that fray easily or have a low thread count. I describe two types of appliqué in this section. *Needle-turn appliqué* is when the shape being "applied" to the background has its seam allowance folded toward the back and tucked underneath the shape. This creates a nice finish. Materials that are thicker and therefore harder to fold a small edge with would be better suited for a *raw-edge appliqué* technique.

The Fence Line Quilt (page 105) incorporates Dresden Fans as well as Dresden Plates as appliqué elements.

TEMPLATES & RELATED TOOLS

In theory you can cut any shape you like and perform either needle-turn or raw-edge appliqué onto a background with or without the use of a form or template to make them regular. I think that improvisational appliqué is stunning. While I indulge in that from time to time, I most often write patterns where the quilter using them can replicate what I have made. Therefore, offering specific shapes to cut and sew is a regular part of my design process. But there is no limit to the combinations you can make even with the same template shapes.

Here are some tools to keep on hand for use alongside the appliqué templates in this book:

- Sharp pencil and fine-line Sharpie
- Quilter's template plastic
- Sharp craft scissors for cutting plastic
- Fabric scissors or a small rotary cutter and mat
- Tin foil sheets from the grocery

The appliqué templates provided at the end of this book have two lines on the edge of the shape. The inner line represents the shape's size once it is completed with needle-turn appliqué and the outer line represents the cut size of the fabric. Should you wish to use raw edge appliqué, the inner line would be your cut line.

All appliqué shapes go through various preparatory steps before they can be sewn into place. That preparation varies depending on which method you choose. All of the projects in this book can be adapted to suit the method you prefer, so it's a good idea to familiarize yourself with each process if you're new to appliqué as it might help you to decide what to try.

NEEDLE-TURN APPLIQUÉ

My favorite method of appliqué is needle turn by hand. There are many ways to achieve this, and each method comes with its own set of tools or notions. I really like when something is straightforward and I generally use one of these two shape-preparation methods. You can use either of them to perform the needle-turn appliqué projects in this book.

STARTING WITH A PRESSED, FOLDED EDGE:

The folded edge of your shape can be created by creasing it with your iron. You can do this either against a firm form like interfacing or cardboard that will stay in place, or around template plastic (on a medium iron setting) that will be removed and reused. Here are some steps to create the form from the templates in this book.

1. Lay the template plastic over the shape you want to use and carefully trace it with a fine-line Sharpie. This will be the inner line of the shape with this book's templates.

2. Cut the shape out on the traced line using craft scissors and as accurately as you can.

In order to create a shape from the fabric with a smooth creased edge that is ready to be stitched into place on the background, follow these steps.

1. Create another plastic template form of the same shape; however, this time use the outer line of the shape to trace and cut.

2. Cut the fabric using this larger template using a small rotary cutter. (You can also pencil trace onto the fabric, then cut with scissors if you prefer.)

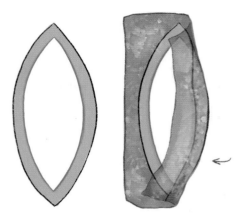

Fig. 1

3. Tear a small piece of tin foil a few inches larger in both directions than your fabric shape. Place the fabric shape onto the foil in the center, with the wrong side facing up. Place the smaller template against the wrong side of your fabric in the center so that you're revealing the ¼" (6 mm) seam allowance all around the edges.

Scan to watch a tutorial.

4. Use the tin foil to fold over and wrap the seam allowances over the edges of the form all around (*Fig. 1*). Continue to smooth the foil edge with your fingers, which is the first step to creating a crease.

5. Next use the heat of an iron, just on the outer edge, to press the foil shape. Let cool and remove the foil and form to reveal your fresh crease.

Creases have a way of falling out over time, so it's easiest to work with a fresh one. For this reason, I like to press each shape one by one, or only a few at a time, just before I begin sewing it in place. I use this method before I begin hand appliqué, although you could alternately machine appliqué with a blanket stitch or your favorite decorative stitch. Whether by machine or by hand, I like to dab a bit of glue stick onto the back of the shape and place as desired before sewing rather than using pins.

STARTING WITH A MACHINE-BASTED EDGE:

Scan to watch a tutorial.

Another method I enjoy is one that starts with machine-basting the shapes in place. For this method, you only need to cut the fabric on the larger outer line of the template. Machine-baste ¼" (6 mm) away from the raw edge against the background fabric. Then, as you hand appliqué the shape in place, you can remove an inch or so of basting stitches first as you go around *(Fig. 2)*. There are more notes on this in the Stitching section at right.

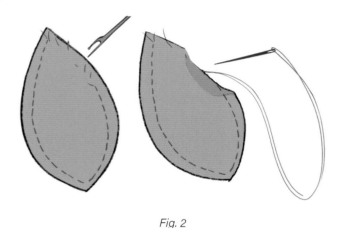

Fig. 2

I particularly enjoy this method because it eliminates the need for pins or glue during the stitching, your shape stays in place as you stitch, and the work is more comfortable and portable. Also, the perforation caused by the machine needle during the basting (in both the shape and the background) helps to see where to fold the shape and stitch in place. The perforation also helps the fabric to fold more easily.

THE STITCHING

Scan to watch a tutorial.

If you have ever performed a blind stitch by hand to whip down a quilt binding, then you have essentially already learned to appliqué. There are of course some nuances to curved shapes that do not exist on a straight binding.

Keep the following supplies on hand for my methods of needle-turn appliqué sewing:

- Small embroidery needles (I like the sharpness and easy-to-thread eyes)
- Thread snips
- Seam ripper (if your pieces are basted)
- Glue stick for any shape repositioning
- Whatever thread you like for machine sewing

Double threading the needle and knotting a length that is about fingertips-to-elbow prevents the tail from slipping through the eye and tangling.

If a crease is already pressed, but has become lax, you may have to use the tip of your needle to drag the seam allowance edge back under as you stitch. When making the first stitch, start from underneath the background fabric and come out through the folded edge of the shape. Stitches (about ⅛" [3.2 mm] long) alternate between picking up a bit of background, then a bit of shape, always coming out just barely underneath the fold of the shape, and back into the background *(Fig. 3)*. It is a process of letting the needle meander through both seam allowance and background continuously and invisibly. More practice will allow you to pick up several stitches at a time. I tend to work with the piece flat on a table, without a hoop, and use the fingertips of my nonworking hand on the top of the appliqué piece to keep the shape secure as I stitch with the other hand.

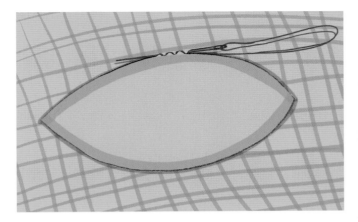

Fig. 3

If the edges are basted first, after lifting out the stitches you will be folding (dragging seam allowance under with the tip of the needle) on the previously basted line as you stitch using the same technique. If necessary, you can additionally secure tricky parts as you go with pins or a glue stick if it helps your process.

With either method, once you have worked around the shape and reached the first stitches made, you can slip the needle to the back side. Finish threads on the wrong side of the background by making a few tacking stitches safely behind an appliqué piece, knotting and trimming.

RAW-EDGE APPLIQUÉ

As the name might imply, pieces cut for raw-edge appliqué will not need any seam allowance added, but rather can be traced on the inner line of each template shape. However, you will likely want to secure that raw edge from fraying, and my favorite way to do that is by first backing the fabric with a fusible interfacing. I use sheer fusible interfacing (Pellon® 805 Wonder-Under®, to be specific). This product does well at securing the raw edges, especially if pressed to the whole fabric wrong side before cutting.

Machine stitching raw edges of shapes that have been fused into place is considerably less time-consuming than performing the work by hand.

Here are the steps I use to get a single-shape fussy cut from fabric and prepared for sewing:

1. Use a pencil to trace the template shape to the paper backing of the fusible interfacing.

2. Cut the fusible shape out, leaving a small border around the traced line. It can be imperfect.

3. Lay the fusible side of the shape against the wrong side of the fabric and center the traced lines precisely over the part of the fabric design you want to appear in your shape.

4. Press firmly into place with an iron; no steam necessary.

5. Cut the piece out of the fused fabric carefully on your traced line *(Fig. 4)*.

(continued)

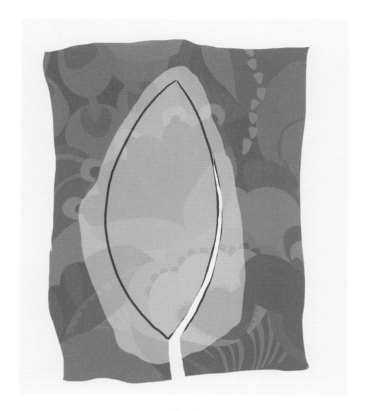

Fig. 4

Fig. 5

Here are the steps I use to get multiple shapes from the same fabric, with no fussy cutting:

1. Press a large piece of fusible interfacing onto the wrong side of the fabric (a fat quarter or larger).

2. Trace all the shapes you want with a pencil onto the paper backing of the fused fabric.

3. Cut the shapes out carefully on the traced lines.

When it's time to fuse the shapes onto your desired background, you can score the paper backing with the tip of a straight pin to begin peeling off the paper and discarding. Position the shape as desired onto the background and press well with an iron to fuse.

When doing raw-edge appliqué with a fusible product, I always use the machine to stitch the pieces in place (Fig. 5). Fusing down all the shapes eliminates the need for pins or basting. Take some time to explore any decorative stitches on your machine and adjust the width and length to see what you might like to use. When using a decorative stitch, the machine needle drops in two or more positions across the width to create the design. When I pass my appliqué shape under the needle of decorative stitching, I am always sure to let the farthest outside needle position of the design fall into the background fabric and let the rest of them fall into the appliqué shape. I avoid letting the needle drop right into the very edge of the shape because I don't want to encourage fraying by splitting the edge.

Scan to watch a tutorial.

CURVED STRIPS WITH BIAS

Scan to watch a tutorial.

If you have previously cut fabric strips for binding on the bias (the 45-degree angle) of the fabric, then you only have a few more steps before you're creating curvy lines for appliqué. My favorite way to introduce curves in a quilt is usually with strips or stems that support an appliqué flower. The following tutorial will take you through cutting, pressing, curving, and sewing a curved stem into place.

1. To easily find the bias angle of your fabric, lay out a piece (even as small as a fat quarter) on your cutting mat with the selvage edge at your right and left. Take the top right corner of the fabric and fold it over itself as though you're dog-earing a book page but keep dragging that corner toward the lower cut edge. Stop when the right selvage edge is in line with the bottom cut line.

2. The angled fold that you see is the perfect 45-degree angle and therefore the bias. Lay a long cutting grid over the angle, until just a sliver of the fold edge is revealed, and trim to achieve a clean edge. You can now cut any width of strips you would like (I usually cut 1½" for stems) from that edge. Leaving fabric double will yield two strips with each cut.

3. You can join strips at a right angle and trim off seam allowance to create the desired length *(Fig. 6)*.

4. With one strip, press a ¼" (6 mm) of seam allowance back toward the wrong side on both long edges.

5. To curve the strip, carefully run the iron with one hand over the strip with your other hand out ahead of the iron pulling on one edge to stretch it. The outer edge of the curve will need the most stretching, so consider that as you encourage a turn in the bias with the pulling and pressing. A very steep curve will need several passes of repeating this process.

The Time Travel Quilt (page 163) uses curved strips with bias as the main feature of the design.

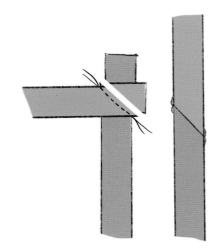

Fig. 6

MORE TECHNIQUES

ENGLISH PAPER PIECING

English Paper Piecing is a beautiful tradition of hand-piecing various geometric shapes together in a plethora of arrangements to create visually exciting outcomes. Usually created from shapes like hexagons, pentagons, triangles, and diamonds, this piecework is traditionally relatively small in scale. English Paper Piecing (often just referred to as EPP), as the name implies, comes together with the use of firm paper forms in your desired shapes that are wrapped with fabric pieces in order to maintain precision of shape. Only after each shape is wrapped and thread tacked do you begin to piece these shapes together one by one by hand with tiny stitches. The papers are easily removed when you

have completed a desired unit of EPP for appliqué or when you have created a quilt top all from EPP.

It might sound tedious, but if you like handwork, you might catch the EPP bug after your first try! It took me years of quilting before I added it to my repertoire, but I have developed a real love for the meditative process, much like my love for crochet and embroidery.

COLLAGE

As I mentioned earlier, my creative career began as an art student studying painting and drawing. It might not be surprising that my favorite elective courses in art school were mixed media fiber courses that I took in the very small textiles department. This is where I was first introduced to many forms of fiber art, among them textile collage. I was simply enamored with the idea of turning a photo into a puzzle of shapes and then rebuilding that puzzle with various printed fabrics. I was inspired by some outcomes that are very cubist in their style and others that are very painterly. Again it is an art form that can be tedious, but is as full of visual opportunity as any fine art medium. In essence these collages are patchworks. Whether or not these patchworks of various fabrics include sewing or even a single stitch, the resulting collage can be an enticing exploration of color and form.

We will veer off into the collage-making process in the final project in the book, Adjusting Her Crown Collage (page 175).

We venture into some EPP with the Sheer Delight Window Panel (page 87).

FINISHING SCHOOL

This book is focused on the color and design side of my process, so we won't delve into all of the techniques involved with layering, basting, quilting, and binding your quilt. However, there are a plethora of resources online and in other more basic quilt books to help you make decisions and perform various finishing methods for your quilt. It is, however, a good idea to have an idea of whether you will be tackling the quilting yourself, by either hand or machine, or whether you will be hiring a long-arm quilter. Some of these decisions might affect other choices in your quilt-making process. Therefore, all the projects simply instruct making the quilt top.

As much as I love to spend hour after hour hand quilting, I would have time for little else if I did not also employ the help of a long-arm machine quilter from time to time. I consider myself lucky to know the quilters I work with personally. While your local quilt shop can often pass along references for a quilting service, it is always a good idea to have one recommended based on first-hand experience. If you are hiring someone for the first time, perhaps start with a smaller simpler project to make sure they are a good fit for your needs.

Hand quilting the Terrace Views Quilt (page 113) was a joyful process.

The Blueprints

3

It is time to build the quilt of your dreams, and I have drafted dreamy blueprints for you to support the process. These four Blueprint chapters will each move and shift through four different projects to provide joyful variations on a theme. The first quilt in each blueprint will be the most beginner friendly, the second more intermediate, and the third will require the most time and technique skill. Finally, each blueprint will have a fourth, tangential project that follows the same structural notes, but we'll create fashionable patchwork art and accessories for you, your home, and even for baby.

1

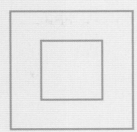

GRAND CENTRAL

The square is perhaps the most basic of all shapes and a perfect place to start when building patchwork design skills. As regular and simplistic as it seems, creating various border styles that work themselves concentrically around a central square offers an opportunity to create some captivating quilts. With balance on our side, we will work our way through some basic but also less predictable paths toward the Grand Central Blueprint.

DO-SI-DO QUILT

As the name implies, I created this quilt design like a dance—a square dance! Using nothing but humble squares, I decided that setting them on point offers a bit more interest and movement. No one section of the quilt overwhelms another, and the mostly small-scale prints are only every now and then interrupted with larger-scale prints. The color borders interlace together to give you something to appreciate at every distance.

COLOR NOTES

While these color choices are somewhat primary by using shades of red, blue, and yellow, the outer border adds shades of plum and lavender. Essentially each of these four colors shows up in three value versions so they can emulate a gingham. Whether you use the same or different four colors, be sure to choose light, medium, and dark versions of each. You can vary the fabric choices as much as you like to suit your scrappy desires.

Size: 70" (177.8 cm) square

Block Size: 3½" (8.9 cm) finished

Building Block: Square

Technique: Machine Patchwork

Skill Level: Beginner

FABRICS

Fat eighth of dark red

Fat eighth of medium red

Fat eighth of light red

⅓ yard (30.5 cm) of dark blue

½ yard (45.7 cm) of medium blue

½ yard (45.7 cm) of light blue

½ yard (45.7 cm) of dark yellow

¾ yard (68.6 cm) of medium yellow

1 yard (91.4 cm) of light yellow

¾ yard (68.6 cm) of dark purple

1¼ yards (114.3 cm) of medium purple

1 yard (91.4 cm) of light purple

(continued)

CUTTING

All squares are cut at 4" (10.2 cm). Note that due to the small size of the squares, I chose to cut all pieces as squares first and then trim the outside edges to triangles at the end of the assembly steps.

1. Cut five dark red squares.

2. Cut four medium red squares.

3. Cut four light red squares.

4. Cut twenty dark blue squares.

5. Cut thirty-two medium blue squares.

6. Cut thirty-two light blue squares.

7. Cut thirty-six dark yellow squares.

8. Cut sixty-four medium yellow squares.

9. Cut sixty-four light yellow squares.

10. Cut fifty-two dark purple squares.

11. Cut ninety-six medium purple squares.

12. Cut seventy light purple squares.

SEWING & ASSEMBLY

Since all of the blocks for this quilt are essentially created from the moment they are cut as simple squares, the sewing and assembly steps are one and the same. The assembly map at right shows you the layout of the quilt by its twelve color categories (four colors in three values). We will assemble the quilt in a total of twenty-seven diagonal rows.

1. Sew one square to another to the next to make the long center row, carefully following the order of color. Press all seam allowances in one direction.

2. Sew the next row (to either the right or left of the center row) in the same manner. Press this row's seam allowances all in the opposite direction of the first.

3. Continue to assemble rows toward the corner of the quilt; the rows will be ever decreasing in length. Continue to alternate the pressing direction of their seam allowances so that the rows nest together neatly in assembly.

4. Once you have worked your way out to the corner of the quilt, repeat the process to make the remaining rows for the other side of the quilt.

5. When all of the diagonal rows are assembled, begin sewing one row to the next, matching the seam intersections. Pin the rows together before sewing if it helps. Continue until the top is assembled.

6. With a straight edge, trim off all of the triangular edges around the perimeter of the quilt top so that you're left with straight edges. Be sure to trim these outer rows of squares ¼" (6 mm) to the outside of the center to leave yourself a seam allowance space for binding.

7. Give the quilt top a good pressing before quilting and binding as desired.

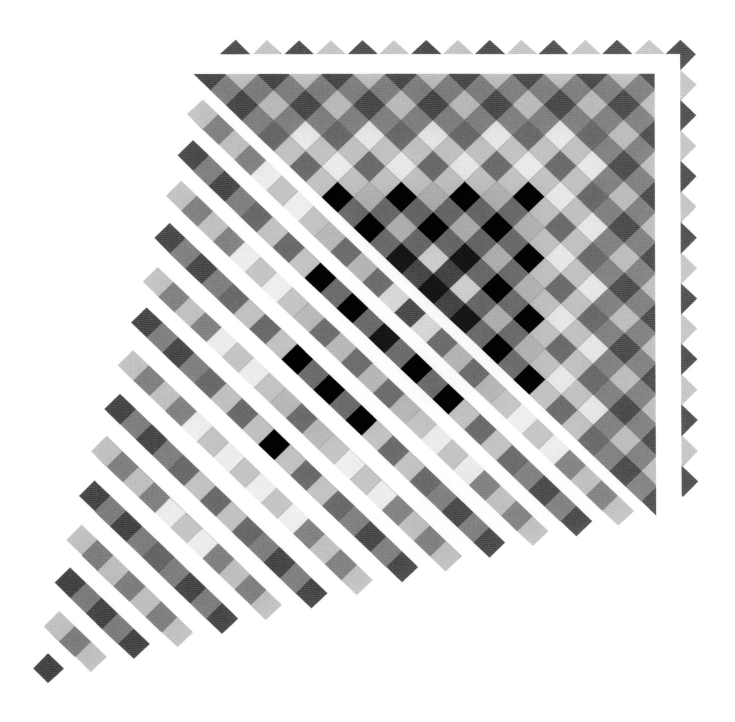

Assembly Map

(continued)

Grand Central Blueprint

HEDGEROW QUILT

In the Hedgerow Quilt, I have satisfied a long-desired approach to the Log Cabin Block by passing color change through the blocks themselves rather than segregating blocks by color. The arrangement of these blocks conveys complexity, but the color planning is apparent and simple. I chose to also use the Dresden Fan Blocks in a similar bicolor fashion around the outer edges of the paler blue section for interest.

COLOR NOTES

Of all of the complement pairs, I find red/green the most challenging to experiment with due to worrying it will end up looking too jarring (or Christmassy). I decided to tackle this color story with a soft and earthy approach by using soft blues and aquas as well as pale corals and peach tones. Beyond organizing the concentric borders by color, I also used value and intensity to increase the drama and interest of the design.

....

Size: 85" (215.9 cm) square

....

Block Size: 12" (30.5 cm) finished

....

Building Blocks: Log Cabin, Dresden Plate, Dresden Fan

....

Templates: Medium Petal, Large Petal, Medium Circle

....

Techniques: Machine Piecing and Appliqué

....

Skill Level: Intermediate

....

FABRICS

The yardage requirements for this quilt are more by general color and value category than they are specific and include only a few fussy-cut fabrics or design elements. Treat this as an opportunity to organize some of your scraps as well as some larger cuts in your fabric collection. The variety or uniformity is completely up to you.

For Log Cabins (very scrappy):

1 to 2 yards (91.4 cm to 182.9 cm) of assorted dark and intense red/coral/orange prints

Up to ½ yard (45.7 cm) of medium red/coral/orange prints

Up to 2 yards (182.9 cm) or more of assorted pale coral/red/pink/orange prints

Up to 2 yards (182.9 cm) or more of assorted medium blue/aqua/green prints

Up to 2 yards (182.9 cm) or more of assorted pale blue/aqua/green prints

For Dresden Plate and Dresden Fans (more specific):

Assorted scraps for center Dresden Plate petals

1¼ yards or more (114.3 cm or more) of medium green print for whole background

¾ yard (68.6 cm) of deep red print for whole background

Twelve floral elements for fussy-cut flower circles

1¼ yards (114.3 cm) of dark green print for setting triangles

½ yard (45.7 cm) of feature print for corner triangles

Assorted medium green/aqua scraps for Large Petal blocks H

Assorted pale blue/green/aqua scraps for Large Petal blocks I

(continued)

CUTTING

To help with organization, we will cut by the nine different block designs labeled A through I. Note that for log cabin cutting all strips are 2" (5.1 cm) wide, so the size will be offered in length only. For each color category noted below, you can precut 2" (5.1 cm) × WOF strips first before sub-cutting into lengths.

1. For block A, cut:
   - one 12½" (31.8 cm) square from medium green
   - twelve assorted Medium Petals
   - 1 Medium Circle

2. For blocks B, cut:
   - four 3½" (8.9 cm) squares from medium red/coral/orange
   - from dark red/coral/orange, cut the following lengths from the 2" (5.1 cm) strips:
     ‣ four 6½" (16.5 cm) / four 9½" (24.1 cm) / four 12½" (31.8 cm)
   - from pale red/coral/orange, cut the following lengths from the 2" (5.1 cm) strips:
     ‣ four 3½" (8.9 cm) / eight 5" (12.7 cm) / four 6½" (16.5 cm) / eight 8" (20.3 cm) / four 9½" (24.1 cm) / eight 11" (27.9 cm)

3. For blocks C, cut:
   - four 3½" (8.9 cm) squares from medium red/coral/orange
   - from pale red/coral/orange, cut the following lengths from the 2" (5.1 cm) strips:
     ‣ four 5" (12.7 cm) / four 6½" (16.5 cm) / four 8" (20.3 cm) / four 9½" (24.1 cm) / four 11" (27.9 cm) / four 12½" (31.8 cm)
   - from medium blue/aqua/green, cut the following lengths from the 2" (5.1 cm) strips:
     ‣ four 3½" (8.9 cm) / four 5" (12.7 cm) / four 6½" (16.5 cm) / four 8" (20.3 cm) / four 9½" (24.1 cm) / four 11" (27.9 cm)

4. For blocks D, cut:
   - four 3½" (8.9 cm) squares from medium red/coral/orange
   - from pale red/coral/orange, cut the following lengths from the 2" (5.1 cm) strips:
     ‣ four 6½" (16.5 cm) / four 9½" (24.1 cm) / four 12½" (31.8 cm)
   - from medium blue/aqua/green, cut the following lengths from the 2" (5.1 cm) strips:
     ‣ four 3½" (8.9 cm) / eight 5" (12.7 cm) / four 6½" (16.5 cm) / eight 8" (20.3 cm) / four 9½" (24.1 cm) / eight 11" (27.9 cm)

5. For blocks E, cut:
   - four 3½" (8.9 cm) squares from medium red/coral/orange
   - from medium blue/aqua/green, cut the following lengths from the 2" (5.1 cm) strips:
     ‣ four 5" (12.7 cm) / four 6½" (16.5 cm) / four 8" (20.3 cm) / four 9½" (24.1 cm) / four 11" (27.9 cm) / four 12½" (31.8 cm)
   - from pale blue/aqua/green, cut the following lengths from the 2" (5.1 cm) strips:
     ‣ four 3½" (8.9 cm) / four 5" (12.7 cm) / four 6½" (16.5 cm) / four 8" (20.3 cm) / four 9½" (24.1 cm) / four 11" (27.9 cm)

6. For blocks F, cut:
   - four 3½" (8.9 cm) squares from medium red/coral/orange
   - from medium blue/aqua/green, cut the following lengths from the 2" (5.1 cm) strips:
     ‣ four 6½" (16.5 cm) / four 9½" (24.1 cm) / four 12½" (31.8 cm)
   - from pale blue/aqua/green, cut the following lengths from the 2" (5.1 cm) strips:
     ‣ four 3½" (8.9 cm) / eight 5" (12.7 cm) / four 6½" (16.5 cm) / eight 8" (20.3 cm) / four 9½" (24.1 cm) / eight 11" (27.9 cm)

(continued)

Grand Central Blueprint

7. For blocks G, cut:
   - four 3½" (8.9 cm) squares from medium red/coral/orange
   - from pale blue/aqua/green, cut the following lengths from the 2" (5.1 cm) strips:
     - four 3½" (8.9 cm) / four 6½" (16.5 cm) / four 9½" (24.1 cm)
   - from dark red/coral/orange, cut the following lengths from the 2" (5.1 cm) strips:
     - eight 5" (12.7 cm) / four 6½" (16.5 cm) / eight 8" (20.3 cm) / four 9½" (24.1 cm) / eight 11" (27.9 cm) / four 12½" (31.8 cm)

8. For blocks H, cut:
   - four 12½" (31.8 cm) squares from deep red
   - twelve Large Petals from medium green/aqua
   - eight Large Petals from different medium green/aqua

9. For blocks I, cut:
   - eight 12½" (31.8 cm) squares from medium green
   - twenty-four Large Petals from pale blue/green/aqua
   - sixteen Large Petals from different pale blue/green/aqua

10. For all Dresden Fan Blocks, fussy cut twelve Medium Circles on a similar floral element.

11. For setting triangles, cut eight 13½" (34.3 cm) squares from the dark green print, then sub-cut them on the diagonal for a total of sixteen triangles.

12. For corner triangles, cut two 8½" (21.6 cm) squares, then sub-cut both on the diagonal for a total of four triangles.

SEWING

For all sewing, refer to the key of blocks that details the color arrangement of the strips.

1. For A, create a Dresden Plate using your desired arrangement of Medium Petals, and appliqué it to the center of the background square. Carefully trim out the background if desired before appliquéing the Medium Circle over the center. Press well.

2. For all B blocks, use the illustration to sew four Log Cabin Blocks in the prescribed color arrangement. Press well.

3. For all C blocks, use the illustration to sew four Log Cabin Blocks in the prescribed color arrangement. Press well.

4. For all D blocks, use the illustration to sew four Log Cabin Blocks in the prescribed color arrangement. Press well.

5. For all E blocks, use the illustration to sew eight Log Cabin Blocks in the prescribed color arrangement. Press well.

6. For all F blocks, use the illustration to sew four Log Cabin Blocks in the prescribed color arrangement. Press well.

7. For all G blocks, use the illustration to sew four Log Cabin Blocks in the prescribed color arrangement. Press well.

8. For all H blocks, use the illustration to sew four Dresden Fans in the prescribed color arrangement and appliqué to background. Wait until after assembly to trim out any background. Press well.

9. For all I blocks, use the illustration to sew eight Dresden Fans in the prescribed color arrangement and appliqué to background. Wait until after assembly to trim out any background. Press well.

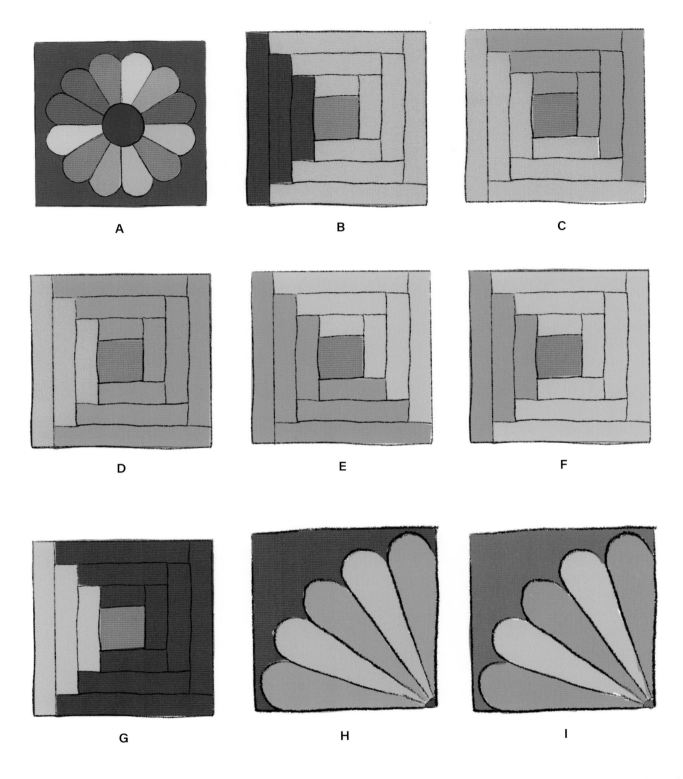

A
B
C
D
E
F
G
H
I

Block Key

(continued)

ASSEMBLY

Use the quilt map labeled with blocks to assemble quilt.

1. Sew one square to another to the next to make the diagonal in the long center row, carefully following the order of color, and the orientation of each block. Both ends of this row require a corner triangle. Press all seam allowances in one direction.

2. Sew the next row that will be stitched to either the right or left of the center row in the same manner. Both ends of this and the following rows will have a setting triangle, so be sure they are oriented the correct way. Press this row's seam allowances all in the opposite direction of the first.

3. Continue to assemble rows toward the corner of the quilt; the rows will be ever decreasing in length. Also continue to alternate the pressing direction of their seam allowances so that they will nest together neatly in assembly.

4. Once you have worked your way out to the corner of the quilt, begin on the other side of center and complete the remaining rows.

5. When all of the diagonal rows are assembled, sew one row to the next, matching the seam intersections. Pin the rows before sewing if it helps. Continue until all rows are assembled and then stitch the last two corner triangles.

6. You can now center each of the twelve fussy-cut circles onto the intersections of four blocks at the narrow points of the Dresden Fans, all around the perimeter of the quilt, and appliqué them in place. Trim out the backgrounds of the H and I blocks if desired.

7. Give the quilt a good pressing before quilting and binding as desired.

Assembly Map

SPONTANEITY QUILT

This Grand Central design is truly that: grand and central. Most of the quilt's space is taken up by a large 9-Patch of Checkerboard Blocks followed by a zigzag border of Half-Square Triangles, followed by a wheel arrangement of Grandmother's Fan Blocks. The repeated use of the same fabric and shape is counterbalanced by a less pre-dictable appliqué border. The wheels at the bottom of the quilt take on floral personalities with stems supporting them and one brave half-wheel even turned upside down to be a flower.

COLOR NOTES

The colors in this quilt rally together in various parts to make themselves bigger and bolder than their simple shapes. Tonal red checkerboards intermingle with tonal orange checkerboards to celebrate analogous color, which is echoed by a complement of a blue-green Half-Square Triangle border. The multicolored floral in the wheels sets the stage for more color experimentation on the borders.

Size: 80" (203.2 cm) square

Block Size: 10" (25.4 cm) and 5" (12.7 cm) finished

Building Blocks: 16-Patch, Grandmother's Fan, Half-Square Triangle, Square

Templates: Long Fan Blade, Large Circle, Large Leaf, Small Oval, Medium Oval

Techniques: Machine Piecing and Appliqué

Skill Level: Intermediate to Advanced

FABRICS

½ yard (45.7 cm) each of deep red and lighter red

½ yard (45.7 cm) each of deep orange and lighter orange

¾ yard (68.6 cm) each of deep blue-green floral and light blue floral

2 yards (182.9 cm) (more or less depending on fussy cutting) of a linear, multicolored floral

4–6 yards (365.8 cm–548.6 cm) (dependent on piecing or not) of neutral background

Eight same elements for fussy cutting blue floral appliqué circles

Assorted cuts or scraps of materials for appliqué borders (a few ½ yard (45.7 cm) or more for cutting bias stem lengths)

Any other desired elements for appliqué (I used some spare English Paper Piecing blocks)

(continued)

PATCHWORK CUTTING

1. For A, cut four 3" (7.6 cm) × WOF strips from deep red and from lighter red fabric.

2. For B, cut four 3" (7.6 cm) × WOF strips from deep orange and from lighter orange fabric.

3. For C, cut:
    - twelve 6" (15.2 cm) squares from deep blue-green floral
    - twelve 6" (15.2 cm) squares from light blue floral

4. For D, cut four 5½" (14 cm) squares from same deep blue-green floral as C.

5. For E, cut:
    - twenty 10½" (26.7 cm) squares from neutral background fabric
    - eighty fussy-cut Long Fan Blades from linear floral fabric

6. For borders, cut two 10½" × 60½" (26.7 × 153.7 cm) and two 10½" × 80½" (26.7 × 204.5 cm) lengths from neutral fabric.

APPLIQUÉ CUTTING

Keep in mind that apart from the circles on the centers of the wheels, the appliqué border design is completely up to you. You could forego the appliqué altogether for a smaller quilt (60" × 60" / 152.4 × 152.4 cm), or replace it with different 10" (25.4 cm) blocks or a single illustrative floral that is begging to be a border. Here are the details of each appliqué element I included in my quilt and the number of each.

1. Eight fussy-cut Medium Circles from blue floral elements (for wheel centers)

2. Forty-six Large Leaves

3. Ten Medium Ovals

4. Twelve Small Ovals

5. 1½" (3.8 cm)-wide bias-cut stems in the following approximate lengths:
    - 75" (190.5 cm) for right continuous (but pieced) right border

- fourteen different cuts ranging from 10" to 20" (25.4 to 50.8 cm) long for bottom and left border
- Seventy-four EPP (English Paper Piecing; see page 60 for more information) hexagons for ten seven-piece flowers and two two-piece stems for top border
- two 1½" (3.8 cm) × 8" (20.3 cm) strips for EPP stems on top border

PATCHWORK SEWING

1. Create five 16-Patch Blocks of deep and light red using the Strip Pieced Block method for A. Press well.

2. Create four 16-Patch Blocks of deep and light orange using the Strip Pieced Block method for B. Press well.

3. Create twenty-four HSTs of deep and light blue green for C blocks. Press well.

4. Create twenty Grandmother's Fan Blocks using the floral blades and neutral squares for E. Save the appliqué circle sewing until after some of the assembly steps. Press well.

Set aside patchwork blocks until assembly.

APPLIQUÉ SEWING

Note that a lot of the appliqué work can be performed on each of the borders before you assemble the quilt top, which will be easier to manage. There are some shapes that you might want to pass over seams between the borders and the center; therefore you can save those pieces for after assembly. I used those "bridging" pieces as a way to disguise inconsistencies of a stem seaming together at a border seam.

1. Prepare your shapes for each border with your desired method of appliqué. If you're following my design, refer to the quilt photo and the assembly map to organize your pieces and lay out the design.

2. Perform the appliqué on each border as desired.

3. Give each border a good press once the appliqué is complete.

(continued)

ASSEMBLY

Use the assembly map labeled with blocks to assemble the center of the quilt.

1. Sew the A blocks and the B blocks together in a 9-Patch arrangement to create the quilt center. Press the seams in alternating directions for a smooth assembly of nested seams.

2. Arrange six of the C blocks in a row forming three light blue peaks and sew them together.

3. Sew this C border to the top edge of the quilt center.

4. Repeat steps 2 and 3 at the bottom of the quilt center.

5. Repeat step 3 for a third C border, but also add D squares to the beginning and end of border. Repeat with the remaining C and D blocks for a fourth C/D border.

6. Sew the C/D borders created in the previous step on the remaining two sides of the quilt center. Make sure that the orientation of the C blocks matches the top and bottom border. Press well.

7. Sew four E blocks together in the orientation shown at the top of the illustration. Repeat with another four E blocks (however, for the bottom of center, you may choose to flip one pair of E blocks as shown).

8. Sew these E borders at the top and bottom of the quilt center, making sure the E curves remain on the outer edge of the quilt center.

9. Sew six E blocks together in a row to create three half circles. Repeat with the remaining E blocks.

10. Sew these E borders at the left and right of the quilt center, making sure the E curves remain on the outer edge of the quilt center. Press well.

11. You can now appliqué eight floral Medium Circles onto the intersections of blocks where the narrow ends of the fan blades meet. If you want to cut out the background from behind the fan blocks (to reduce the weight of the quilt), you can do that now. Press well.

Fig. 1

12. Sew the 60½" (153.7 cm) borders to the right and left side of the quilt center. Press away from the center.

13. Appliqué any further desired appliqué elements over the seams made in the previous step *(Fig. 1)*.

14. Sew the 80½" (204.5 cm) borders to the top and bottom side of the quilt center. Press away from the center.

15. Appliqué any further desired appliqué elements over the seams made in the previous step.

16. Give the quilt a good pressing before quilting and binding as desired.

Assembly Map

SHEER DELIGHT WINDOW PANEL

As much as I have enjoyed peaceful sessions with English Paper Piecing, most of what I have accomplished is several beautiful pieces that are still looking for a home. Enter the Sheer Delight Window Panel where I was inspired to gather three existing EPP elements and appliqué them to a lightweight woven background that lets in a beautiful amount of light. In fact, one of the most beautiful things about hanging an EPP project in a window is that the seams take on a stained-glass effect.

COLOR NOTES

Starting with an existing EPP block meant that the color choices for the other blocks and background were easy. As the existing piece was made of various blue and aqua shades with a charming orange center and black punctuation around the edges, for the other blocks, I chose shades of blue, yellow, orange, pink, and green—with multiple versions of themselves to keep things interesting. I chose a background shade that does not compete with the blocks and allows a pleasing light to shine through it. Test this by just hanging potential background fabric in your window.

Size: 30" × 70" (76.2 × 177.8 cm)

Block Size: 1¼" (3.2 cm)

Building Block: English Paper Piecing

Technique: English Paper Piecing

Skill Level: Advanced Beginner

CONSIDERING YOUR WINDOW

The size of my finished panel is almost identical to the size of my window. If you like the choices I made but have a very different size window, here are a couple ideas of how you could alter the design.

Wider window: Keep the elements the same through the center, but widen the left and right borders to include more flowers instead of just a single line of hexagons.

Shorter window: Make the top and bottom gold flowers smaller, or eliminate them.

Square window: Keep a similar design, but add stems of flowers that grow toward the left and right as well.

Smaller window: Keep elements similar, but sew fewer concentric rows onto the three main flowers in order to make them smaller. Alternately, use smaller EPP hexagons.

Similar but slightly different size: The easiest adjustment is to change the length of the borders.

Simply deciding on your background fabric and cutting a size that matches your window (plus a few inches in both directions) will give you a playground to lay out some of your ideas as you stitch blocks of EPP.

Note: It is a given that your update or alterations to this project would change the fabric requirements, amounts of each color, and therefore directions. However, everything offered here details my exact materials used and process in the hopes that reading through will help with yours.

(continued)

PATCHWORK CUTTING

For all hexagons, use the hexagon paper of your choice as the template, but cut the fabric ¼" larger on all sides. You can most likely find an acrylic template in this shape from wherever you purchased the paper pieces. You can also use template plastic to create your own.

For center flower, cut the following hexagons:

- one dark coral
- six coral
- six turquoise
- six of a different turquoise
- nine light blue
- nine dark blue
- eighteen pale neutral/gray
- six black

For gold flowers, cut the following hexagons:

- six magenta
- twelve bright yellow
- twelve deep gold
- twelve dark gold
- twenty coral/pink
- six green
- eight different green

For borders, cut the following hexagons:

- four black
- twenty-four deep coral
- eight medium coral
- ten gold
- twelve magenta
- forty purple

MATERIALS

Hexagon EPP papers (I used 1¼" [3.2 cm]) (number dependent on your design; I used 235)

A few yards of Pellon® 805 Wonder-Under® (Skip if you prefer hand appliqué.)

Background fabric equal to window size plus 2" (5.1 cm) in both directions (i.e., I cut 32" × 72" [81.3 × 182.9 cm] for 30" × 70" [76.2 × 177.8 cm]) (If window is wider than fabric, use two lengths.)

Rod pocket 4" (10.2 cm) × width of window

Various printed scraps or fat quarters of blue, gray/white, black, orange/coral, yellow/gold, pink/magenta, green

Hand-sewing needle and thread

(continued)

Grand Central Blueprint

EPP BASTING

There are a few different basting methods for wrapping the cut fabric around the papers to prepare them for assembly. You can use glue or needle and thread. I prefer to hand-baste with needle and thread; however, not *through the paper* (that is a different method). It does not matter how you baste as long as you're comfortable with your process.

1. With one hexagon paper against the wrong side of the fabric and centered, first neatly fold one fabric edge over the paper edge, then fold the next edge (clockwise or counterclockwise). Where the two folds overlap at the corner, pass your needle and thread through the fabric fold once (not the paper), and then again to take a whipstitch *(Fig. 1)*. Because the papers are thick, with practice, it becomes easy to only stitch through the fabric and avoid going through the paper.

2. Repeat the fold and whipstitch sequence around in a continuous manner (carrying the thread from one corner to the next) until you have tacked all corners, then knot to finish. Be sure to keep this fabric folding and sewing taut, but not so much that it bends the shape of the hexagon.

3. Repeat the basting for all pieces needed in your design. You should not need an iron to keep these shapes sharply pressed, as the process itself plus a little finger pressing should keep them tidy. I personally like to move on to some assembly of pieces after basting, instead of basting all the project pieces first. This lets me develop the design and be flexible as I go, rather than basting pieces that I don't end up using.

EPP BLOCK SEWING

Assembling the basted fabric/paper shapes together to create a design is a simple task of joining one shape to the next with hand sewing but it can feel a bit finicky at first if you're new to it. Practice will improve your sewing and your comfort level and help to not treat the pieces too preciously. The shapes will recover from any amount of folding required to sew the seams as you build a beautiful design.

1. Once you have laid out the design of a section, begin sewing from the center out. For the central flower, this means sewing the dark coral center together with one of the six lighter coral pieces. With the right sides together (papers left in place) and the edges of hexagon all aligned, begin taking small whipstitches (with a single strand of thread) from one corner to the other of a single side *(Fig. 2)*. These stitches should be tiny and only pick up a couple "threads" of each fabric fold and avoid passing through the paper. I have never measured my stitches but guess they are about 1/16" (1.6 mm) or less apart.

paper

Fig. 1

Anna Maria's Blueprint Quilting

Fig. 2

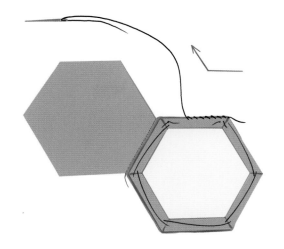

Fig. 3

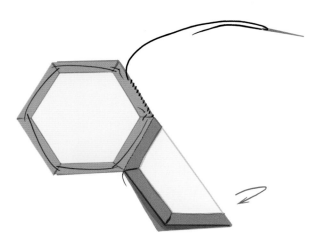

Fig. 4

2. Open the two pieces you just sewed to their right side. Position the next "petal" against the center and next to the first petal. Now put the right sides together of the second petal and center to stitch in the same manner *(Fig. 3)*. You do not need to knot the thread and start again between these shapes but can continue to sew lighter coral pieces all around the six sides of the darker coral center.

3. Next, fold the center hexagon against itself in order to place two of the petals in line to sew the edges between them *(Fig. 4)*. You can either knot to finish each of these seams or sew more continuously to begin adding in the next round of blue pieces as shown in the illustration.

4. Referencing the color map, continue to add all the hexagons necessary to create the central flower. With more practice, the ideal sequence of sewing will become intuitive.

5. Repeat these steps to make the two remaining (gold) flowers.

6. Repeat the steps to make the two small coral flowers (with one green petal) that attach to the gold flower and stem. Add another green piece to the green petal of each flower.

7. Add a row of three green pieces to the top and bottom of the gold flower, extending from the black hexagons, before connecting all the pieces in the cluster to complete the design. This design creates two holes, which you will see the background through.

8. Use the color map to create all of the four border pieces before joining them together.

(continued)

Color Map

APPLIQUÉ SEWING AND FINISHING

You might decide to now hand sew all of the appliqué onto the background, after pinning or glue tacking it into place. I machine-appliquéd my shapes onto the background and used a fusible product to keep them firmly in place as I did. The following instructions detail the process that I used.

1. Finish all edges of the background panel using a folded ½" (13 mm) hem. Press well.

2. Measure and mark the halfway points at the top, bottom, and side edges of the panel with pins.

3. Lay the EPP units onto the paper side of the Pellon® 805 and place a few weights onto them to keep them still. Carefully trace onto the paper all around the whole piece.

4. Cut out the fusible ¼" (6 mm) to the inside of the traced lines. For some of the interior spaces where there is a hole, you might do this more easily with an X-Acto blade.

5. Repeat steps 3 and 4 for all EPP units.

6. Carefully remove all EPP papers from units. Take your time and be gentle with the piece. Press well once they are all removed.

7. Now press the fibrous side of the Pellon® 805 to the wrong side of the EPP unit, making sure it is all aligned within the borders of the shape. Score and peel the paper off the fusible.

8. Using the markings on the panel and paying careful attention to centering, place the fusible side of the EPP unit into position and press into place.

Scan to watch a tutorial.

9. Complete steps 7 and 8 until all appliqué designs are pressed into place.

10. Use a blanket stitch on your sewing machine in a thread color that matches the background panel to sew around the perimeter of all units. Take your time lifting and lowering the machine foot to pivot around the pieces.

11. Once all appliqué sewing is complete, you can turn in all edges of the rod pocket toward the wrong side ½" (1.3 cm) and press well. Sew the two long edges of the pocket at the top edge of the panel by hand (if you want to hide the stitching) or on the machine (Fig. 4). While this will likely go through some of your appliqué, a neutral shade should not be distracting against the colorful prints. Press well.

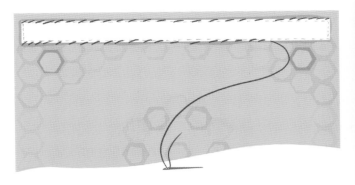

Fig. 4

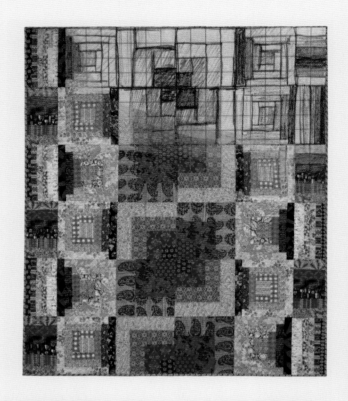

94

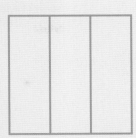

TRIPTYCH

In fine art, a "triptych" is a three-piece work of art that is meant to be viewed as one complete work. Frequently, the center panel is the main panel and the other two are more supportive. But also common is for all three panels to be the exact same size. It was the first title that came to mind for this style of quilt composition that I have revisited many times over the years. I find it to be attractive and foolproof whether you're making simple patchwork or exploding appliqué of all sorts onto a canvaslike background. The left and right sections seem to hold everything pleasantly in place.

ROMAN NUMERALS QUILT

For this first quilt in the Triptych category, there is only a subtle design shift from the center column of patchwork to the side columns. Most of the difference in the sections is the piece size and some color changes. The quilt is also a play on the strip elements of the classic Log Cabin Block. The center blocks are a bit off-kilter because they are Quarter Log Cabins, which are positioned to come together into a full one; however, they have mismatched piece sizes, which creates some playful movement. I named the quilt Roman Numerals because I made it for my son Roman, and because the value shifts in the strip pieces here and there remind me of roman numerals.

COLOR NOTES

When a quilt is made for a loved one, that person often remains on your mind throughout the making process. This quilt had my son Roman and his interests at the forefront of my palette choices. Roman loves world history, flags from various countries, and memorizing the soccer jerseys from teams around the globe. I built upon a classic blue/orange complement story and created interest by shifting through various values of all of these tones. I also chose print styles that are popular in diverse parts of the world from Indian hand-blocked paisleys to more refined stripes and checks.

Size: 60" × 72" (152.4 × 182.9 cm)

Block Size: 12" (30.5 cm) square and 6" × 12" (15.2 × 30.5 cm) finished

Building Blocks: Log Cabin, Quarter Log Cabin, Strip Pieced

Technique: Machine Patchwork

Skill Level: Beginner

(continued)

FABRICS

The fabric requirements are offered by block to help with your planning and organization. Refer to the quilt map to correlate the position of the suggested fabrics.

Block A:

fat quarter of small burgundy

½ yard (45.7 cm) of navy/rust

¾ yard (68.6 cm) of warm paisley

Block B:

fat quarter of black and red

fat quarter of orange

½ yard (45.7 cm) of blue and tan

½ yard (45.7 cm) of gold and cream

Block C:

½ yard (45.7 cm) each of four pale blue fabrics that gradually become darker

½ yard (45.7 cm) each of three more saturated blue/orange

Block D:

(make this a different variety of fabrics from Block C fabrics)

½ yard (45.7 cm) each of four pale blue fabrics that gradually become darker

½ yard (45.7 cm) each of three more saturated blue/orange

Block E:

¼ yard (22.9 cm) each of six different red/gold/rust/burgundy

Block F:

¼ yard (22.9 cm) each of six different blue and aqua

CUTTING

Block A, cut:

- six 4½" (11.4 cm) squares from small burgundy print
- six 4½" (11.4 cm) squares from navy/rust print
- six 4½" × 8½" (11.4 × 21.6 cm) rectangles from navy/rust print
- six 4½" × 8½" (11.4 × 21.6 cm) rectangles from warm paisley print
- six 4½" × 12½" (11.4 × 31.8 cm) rectangles from warm paisley print

Block B, cut:

- six 3½" (8.9 cm) squares from black and red print
- six 3½" (8.9 cm) squares from orange print
- six 3½" × 6½" (8.9 × 16.5 cm) rectangles from orange print
- six 3½" × 6½" (8.9 × 16.5 cm) rectangles from blue and tan print
- six 3½" × 9½" (8.9 × 94.1 cm) rectangles from blue and tan print
- six 3½" × 9½" (8.9 × 94.1 cm) rectangles from gold and cream print
- six 3½" × 12½" (8.9 × 31.8 cm) rectangles from gold and cream print

Block C, cut:

Note the color changes for each of the pieces in the illustration.

- six 3½" (8.9 cm) squares from darkest of pale blues

After first cutting all Block C fabrics into 2" (5.1 cm) × WOF strips, cut the following lengths:

- six 3½" (8.9 cm) and twelve 5" (12.7 cm) from medium blue
- twelve 8" (20.3 cm) from lighter blue
- six 9½" (24.1 cm) and twelve 11" (27.9 cm) from lightest pale blue
- six 6½" (16.5 cm), six 9½" (24.1 cm), and six 12½" (31.8 cm) from more saturated blue and orange fabrics

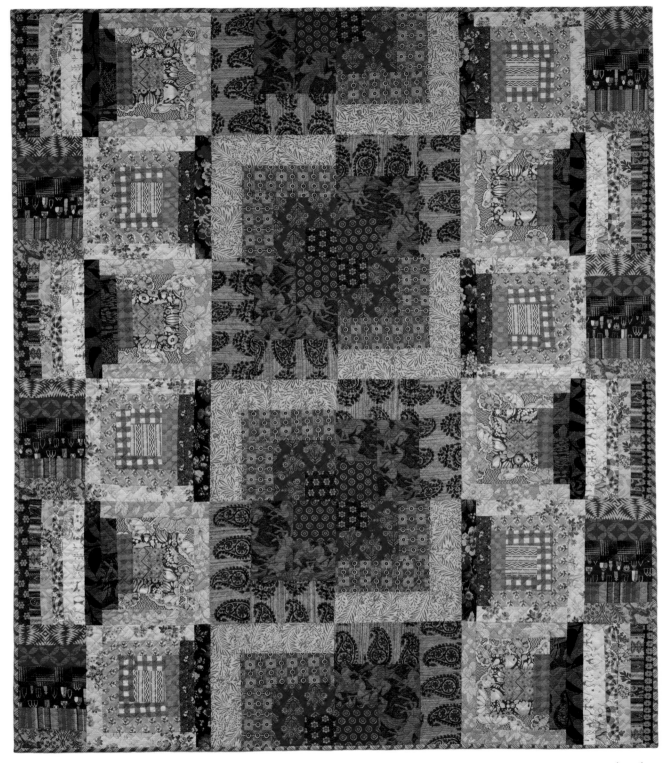

(continued)

Triptych Blueprint

Block D, cut as you did for Block C with the other variety of similar fabrics.

Block E, cut one 2½" (6.4 cm) × WOF strip from each of the red/gold/rust/burgundy fabrics.

Block F, cut two 1½" (3.8 cm) × WOF strips from each of the red/gold/rust/burgundy fabrics.

SEWING

Use the key of blocks to create blocks A through F, making sure to match color and position.

1. For A blocks, sew six Quarter Log Cabin Blocks and press well.

2. For B blocks, sew six Quarter Log Cabin Blocks and press well.

3. For C blocks, sew six Log Cabin Blocks, paying attention to the block key for C.

4. For D blocks, sew six Log Cabin Blocks, paying attention to the block key for D.

5. For E blocks, sew all six WOF strips together on their long edges in your desired order, taking care to keep your ¼" (6 mm) seam allowance consistent. Once all are sewn and pressed well, sub-cut them six times into the final block size of 6½" × 12½" (16.5 × 31.8 cm).

6. For F blocks, sew one of each six WOF strip colors together on their long edges in your desired order, taking care to keep your ¼" (6 mm) seam allowance consistent. Once all are sewn and pressed well, sub-cut them into the final block size of 6½" × 12½" (16.5 × 31.8 cm). You will need to repeat the process again to be able to yield a total of six F blocks.

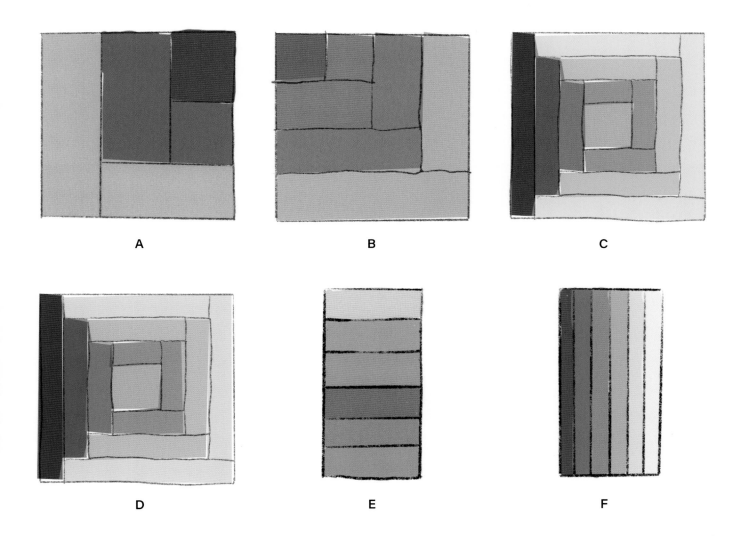

Block Key

(continued)

ASSEMBLY

The assembly map shows you the layout with the blocks marked by their letter. The rows will be assembled vertically.

1. Sew an A block to a B block and continue until one column is complete, taking care to keep the orientation of the blocks the right way. Press all in one direction.

2. Repeat step 1 but instead begin the sequence with a B block and continue until all A and B blocks are assembled.

3. Sew the remaining columns in the same manner (C to D and E to F as shown). Press the subsequent row seam allowances in alternate directions so they nest smoothly together in assembly.

4. Once all of the columns are complete, begin sewing one to the next, matching the seam intersections. Pin the rows before sewing if it helps. Continue until the top is assembled.

5. Give the quilt a good pressing before quilting and binding as desired.

Anna Maria's Blueprint Quilting

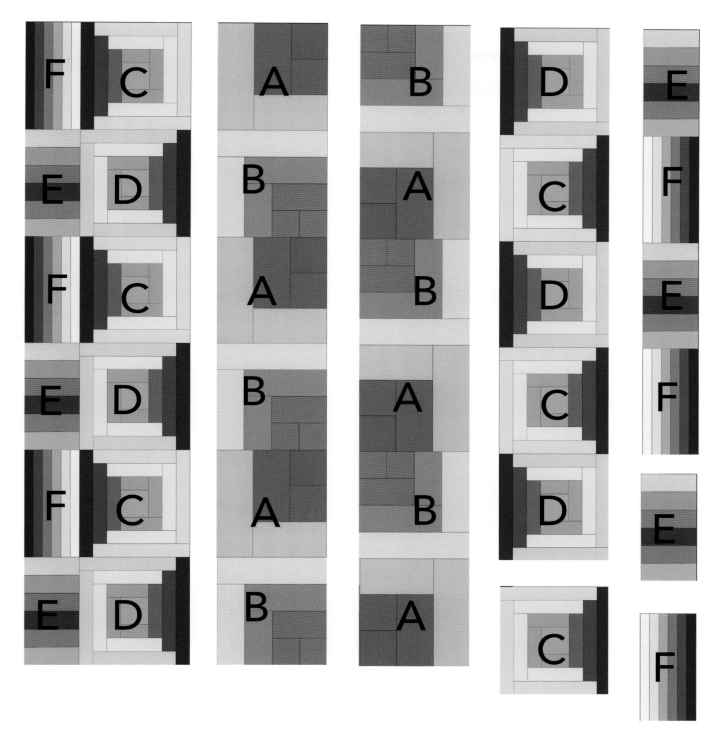

Assembly Map

FENCE LINE QUILT

One of my favorite blocks is the Dresden Plate. While I frequently use them as appliqué flower heads, I thought I would create a canvas of stripes and right angles to set the stage for using the Dresdens in full circle plates as well as using fewer "blades" to create fans of various sizes. The result is somewhere between flowers popping through a picket fence and a more structural cog and wheel composition. The interesting thing about the assembly of this quilt is that it is built with three main horizontal panels but achieves a vertical panel design.

COLOR NOTES

The palette of the quilt is very colorful, but I feel the most notable conversation is between blues and corals. These show up in both soft and more intense versions of themselves. The blues stray into green and aqua territory whereas the corals wander off into vibrant orange and pink territory. The triptych layout is mostly achieved through the use of the vertical color changes that happen on either side of center. The value of the blues and greens also deepens on the far right and left border of the blocks, allowing the warmth in the center to glow.

Size: 63" × 81" (160 × 205.7 cm)

Block Size: 9" (22.9 cm) square

Building Blocks: Quarter Log Cabin, Strip Pieced, Dresden Plate, Dresden Fan

Templates: Small, Medium, Large, and Extra Large Dresden Blade; Medium and Large Circle; Medium Oval

Techniques: Machine Patchwork and Appliqué

Skill Level: Intermediate

FABRICS

The fabric requirements are presented for the Middle and Top/Bottom (which are identical) sections separately, as well as for the appliqué features to help with your planning and organization. Refer to the section quilt maps to correlate the position of suggested fabrics.

MIDDLE SECTION:

nine fat quarters total of assorted coral/orange/pink/yellow

fat quarter of pale aqua

fat quarter of deep green

½ yard (45.7 cm) of blue/purple

¾ yard (68.6 cm) of deep blue

½ yard (45.7 cm) of pale blue

(continued)

TOP / BOTTOM SECTIONS:

If your amounts allow, fabrics can overlap some with previous section.

½ yard (45.7 cm) of nine different orange/pink/yellow/coral

½ yard (45.7 cm) of pale jade/aqua

½ yard (45.7 cm) of pale purple

½ yard (45.7 cm) of deep green

½ yard (45.7 cm) of deep blue

½ yard (45.7 cm) two different illustrative purple

½ yard (45.7 cm) of deep purple

½ yard (45.7 cm) of black

Appliqué Elements:

The appliqué pieces and their coloration will be best chosen once you have decided on your background pieces; you will want some contrast in intensity and color. Choose fat quarters of at least twelve to sixteen different colors including intense yellows, black, purple, burgundy, pink, and green. Some of the scraps from the background fabrics can be included and strategically placed to maintain some unity.

CUTTING

The cutting is organized by block label and section. Organize cut pieces the same way.

MIDDLE SECTION:

1. For A blocks, cut 9½" (24.1 cm) squares in the following amounts and in the following colors:
    *   seven from assorted orange/pink/yellow/coral
    *   two from pale aqua

2. For B blocks, cut 2" (5.1 cm)-wide strips from deep green, deep blue, and pale blue in the following lengths:
    *   deep green: six 9½" (24.1 cm)
    *   deep blue: six 9½" (24.1 cm)
    *   pale blue: six 9½" (24.1 cm)

3. For C blocks, cut 2" (5.1 cm)-wide strips of purple/blue prints (and more of deep blue, if necessary) in the following lengths:
    *   purple/blue: four 2" (5.1 cm), four 3½" (8.9 cm), four 5" (12.7 cm), four 6½" (16.5 cm), four 8" (20.3 cm)
    *   deep blue: six 2" (5.1 cm), six 3½" (8.9 cm), six 5" (12.7 cm), six 6½" (16.5 cm), six 8" (20.3 cm), six 9½" (24.1 cm)
    *   pale blue: two 2" (5.1 cm), two 3½" (8.9 cm), two 5" (12.7 cm), two 6½" (16.5 cm), two 8" (20.3 cm)

4. For D blocks, cut:
    *   deep blue: two 2" × 9½" (5.1 × 24.1 cm) rectangles
    *   gold/orange: two 9½" (24.1 cm) squares

(continued)

Triptych Blueprint

TOP / BOTTOM SECTIONS:

There are two identical top/bottom sections, which are reflected in cutting.

1. For A blocks, cut 9½" (24.1 cm) squares in the following amounts and colors:
   - eight pink/coral/orange/yellow
   - four illustrative purple print
   - two deep blue

2. For B blocks, cut 2" (5.1 cm)-wide strips from deep green, deep blue, and purple in the following lengths:
   - deep green: six 9½" (24.1 cm)
   - deep blue: twelve 9½" (24.1 cm)
   - pale purple: six 9½" (24.1 cm)

3. For C blocks, cut 2" (5.1 cm)-wide stripes from deep purple and black in the following lengths:
   - purple/blue: two 2" (5.1 cm), two 3½" (8.9 cm), two 5" (12.7 cm), two 6½" (16.5 cm), two 8" (20.3 cm)
   - black: two 2" (5.1 cm), two 3½" (8.9 cm), two 5" (12.7 cm), two 6½" (16.5 cm), two 8" (20.3 cm), two 9½" (24.1 cm)

4. For E blocks, cut:
   - two 9½" (24.1 cm) square from gold print
   - two 2" × 9½" (5.1 × 24.1 cm) strip from deep blue
   - two 2" × 4" (5.1 × 10.2 cm) strip from deep blue

5. For F blocks, cut:
   - two 8" (20.3 cm) squares from deep purple
   - two 2" × 9½" (5.1 × 24.1 cm) strips from purple/blue
   - two 2" × 8" (5.1 × 20.3 cm) strips from deep blue

6. For G blocks, cut 9½" (24.1 cm) squares in the following amounts and colors:
   - two from deep purple
   - two from a different deep purple
   - two from deep green
   - two from pale jade/aqua
   - two from gold
   - two from coral

APPLIQUÉ CUTTING:

Use the illustrations to guide cutting for various Dresden Plates and Fans.

1. For G blocks, use the Small Dresden Blade template to cut:
   - thirty total blades that alternate between two colors of the coral/orange families
   - thirty total blades from assorted colors

2. For G blocks, use the Medium Dresden Blade template to cut:
   - thirty total blades from assorted colors
   - total blades alternating between pale purple and purple/blue (10 each)

3. For floating appliqué, cut:
   - twenty-two Medium Dresden Blades alternating between burgundy and floral (11 each)
   - forty Small Dresden Blades alternating between yellow and orange
   - twenty Extra Large Dresden Blades from assorted colors (I used fve fabrics)

4. For Dresden Plate centers, fussy cut:
   - eight Medium Circles
   - one Large Circle
   - two Medium Ovals

PATCHWORK SEWING

Refer to the section maps for general block color and assembly placement based on my quilt.

MIDDLE SECTION:

1. For B blocks, sew two Strip Pieced Blocks from pale blue/deep blue fabrics. Press well.

2. For B blocks, sew two Strip Pieced Blocks from deep green/deep blue fabrics. Press well.

3. For C blocks, sew four Quarter Log Cabin Blocks from deep blue/purple fabrics. Press well.

4. For C blocks, sew two Quarter Log Cabin Blocks from deep blue/pale blue fabrics. Press well.

5. For D blocks, cut a 2" (5.1 cm) strip off of the 9½" (24.1 cm) square. Sew this strip together with the deep blue strip. Now sew these two strips to the previous square piece, with the blue in the center. Trim block at lower edge so that it finishes at 9½" (24.1 cm). Repeat with the other D block.

6. Use the Middle Section Block Map (below) to assemble the three horizontal rows of seven blocks, making sure to keep their orientation in order. Press the Middle Section and set aside.

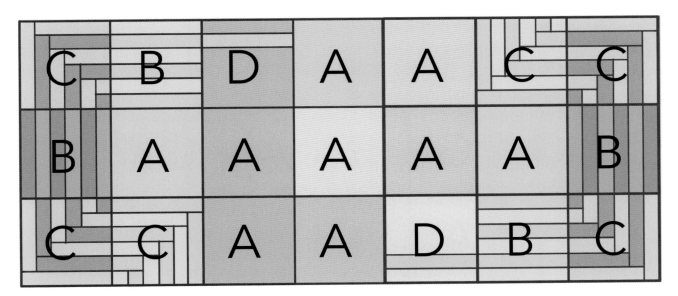

Middle Section Block Map

(continued)

TOP / BOTTOM SECTION:

You will be sewing for two duplicate sections.

1. For B blocks, sew two Strip Pieced Blocks from pale blue/purple fabrics. Press well.

2. For B blocks, sew two Strip Pieced Blocks from deep blue/deep green fabrics. Press well.

3. For C blocks, sew two Quarter Log Cabin Blocks from purple/black fabrics. Press well.

4. For E blocks, cut one square down the center (at 4¾" [12.1 cm]). Sew the 2" × 9½" (5.1 × 24.1 cm) deep blue strip to the long edge of one of the resulting rectangles. Trim the other rectangle to measure 4" × 8" (10.2 × 20.3 cm). Sew the 2" × 4" (5.1 × 10.2 cm) deep blue strip to the top of this rectangle. Now sew it to the other side of the long deep blue strip. Trim E block to 9½" (24.1 cm) square, keeping the long blue strip at the center. Repeat for a second E block.

5. For F block, sew the deep blue strip to one edge of the square. Now sew a purple strip to a perpendicular edge. Trim block to be 9½" (24.1 cm) by cutting off the other two edges of square. Repeat for a second F block.

APPLIQUÉ AND ASSEMBLY SEWING

TOP / BOTTOM SECTION:

1. For G blocks, create three Dresden Fan Blocks using the Small Fan Blades that each have different five-blade colors. Sew them together with a blue/purple B block as shown in the illustration *(Fig. 1)*. Appliqué the Medium Circle over the intersection of these blocks. Repeat for a second four-block unit. Press well, and cut out background behind appliqué if desired.

2. For G blocks, create three Dresden Fan Blocks using the Small Fan Blades that alternate between coral and orange. Sew them together with the F block as shown in the illustration. Appliqué the Medium Circle over the intersection of these blocks. Repeat for a second four-block unit. Press well, and cut out background behind appliqué if desired.

3. For H blocks, sew two Dresden Fan Blocks with medium purple/light purple blades and pale coral background square. Save the oval appliqué until after assembly.

Top/Bottom Section Block Map

Anna Maria's Blueprint Quilting

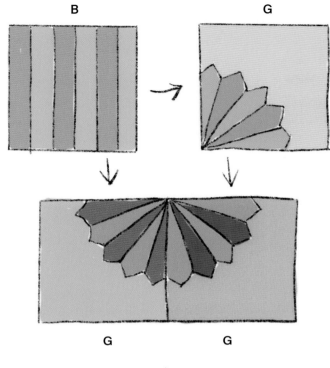

B   G

G   G

Fig. 1

4. For H blocks, sew two Dresden Fan Blocks with medium black/green blades, one on the coral background and one on the light purple background. Repeat for a second pair. Save the circular appliqué until after assembly.

5. Use the Top/Bottom Section Block Map (page 110) to assemble the four-piece units and blocks, keeping an eye on the correct orientation for all elements. Repeat exactly the same way for the Bottom section.

FLOATING APPLIQUÉ:

1. Sew the pale blue circular centers over the narrow ends of the green/black Dresden Fans from the previous step now that the Top/Bottom sections are assembled.

2. Sew the large Dresden Plate from the assorted twenty blades in your desired arrangement. Appliqué this onto the very center of the Middle Section. Then appliqué the large circular center in place at the center of the Dresden. Press well, and cut out the background behind the appliqué if desired.

3. Sew two Dresden Plates from twenty extra-small bright yellow/orange blades. Appliqué these each in place on the Top and Bottom Sections as shown. Also appliqué the medium circular centers. Press well, and cut out the background behind the appliqué if desired.

4. Sew two Dresden Fans from eleven medium floral and burgundy blades. Appliqué these each in place on the Top and the Bottom Sections as shown. Also appliqué the medium oval centers. Press well, and cut out the background behind the appliqué if desired.

5. Finally sew the Top, Middle, and Bottom Sections together, keeping in mind that the Top needs to flip upside down before assembly. Press well and sew the ovals onto the narrow ends of the center H blocks (these are slightly tilted to meet the blue strip from the D block).

6. Give the quilt a final pressing before backing, quilting, and binding as desired.

TERRACE VIEWS QUILT

The Roman Numerals Quilt celebrated a playful approach to right angles and strip piecing. The Fence Line Quilt went a step further by adding the Dresden features albeit formed by straight lines. This Terrace Views Quilt elevates the design variety even further to include not just right angles of patchwork but also diagonals, curves, and an assortment of rhythmic appliqué forms.

COLOR NOTES

This quilt and its palette were inspired by our gorgeous island location of Hydra in Greece when Vince and I married in 2023. The rich ocean blues and the floral highlights along with sunny golds and greens are most of what makes this color story sing. While the arrangement of the elements is very organized and reliable, it is the assorted mix of prints in each color category that makes the quilt a little less predictable.

....

Size: 72" × 90" (182.9 × 228.6 cm)

....

Block Size: 9" (22.9 cm) square

....

Building Blocks: Half-Square Triangle, Snowball, Grandmother's Fan

....

Templates: Small, Medium, and Large Oval; Small and Large Leaf; Large Circle

....

Techniques: Machine Patchwork and Appliqué

....

Skill Level: Intermediate to Advanced

....

FABRICS

Amounts are offered by block to help with your organization.

For A blocks:

⅔ yard (61 cm) of lighter gold/green print

⅔ yard (61 cm) of lighter blue/purple print

For B blocks:

⅔ yard (61 cm) of gold/green print

⅔ yard (61 cm) of blue/purple print

For C, D, and E blocks:

4+ yards (366+ cm) combined of assorted deep blues/turquoise/greens/black/stripes/tonal prints

For C blocks:

eight to ten fat quarters of assorted pink/coral/orange/lavender prints

10 same pink/black floral elements for fussy-cut circles

For D and E blocks:

⅔ yard (61 cm) of deep multicolored purple/blue/magenta small print

For E blocks:

three or four fat quarters of assorted green/aqua prints

Appliqué Elements:

¾ yard (68.6 cm) of aqua print for bias arches

½ yard (45.7 cm) of dull aqua print for small leaves (more or less depending on fussy cutting forty leaves)

twelve or more fat quarters for appliqué including aqua, magenta, bright pink, bright yellow, lime, etc.

(continued)

CUTTING

1. For A blocks, cut ten 10½" (26.7 cm) squares: five from lighter green/gold and five from lighter blue/purple.

2. For B blocks, cut ten 10½" (26.7 cm) squares: five from green/gold and five from blue/purple.

3. For C blocks, cut:
   - twenty 9½" (24.1 cm) squares from assorted deep blue etc. fabrics
   - eighty small Grandmother's Fan Blocks from assorted pink etc. fabrics
   - ten Large Circles from floral elements

4. For D blocks, cut:
   - twenty 9½" (24.1 cm) squares from assorted deep blue etc. fabrics
   - forty 3" (7.6 cm) squares from multicolored purple/blue/magenta small print

5. For E blocks, cut:
   - twenty 9½" (24.1 cm) squares from assorted deep blue etc. fabrics
   - forty 3" (7.6 cm) squares from multicolored purple/blue/magenta small print
   - twenty 5" (12.7 cm) squares from assorted green/aqua prints

APPLIQUÉ CUTTING

1. Cut ten 1½" × 24" (3.8 × 61 cm) bias strips for arches.
   - Cut forty Small Leaves from dull aqua print (fussy cut if desired).

2. From assorted pinks (or Fan scraps), cut:
   - eight Small Leaves from pale pink
   - eight Large Leaves from bright pink
   - sixteen Small Leaves pink/purple

3. From fat quarters, for floating appliqué units in center row, cut:

APPLIQUÉ 1:
   one Large Circle
   two same Medium Ovals
   four same Medium Ovals
   four same Small Ovals

APPLIQUÉ 2:
   two same Large Ovals
   four same Medium Ovals
   eight same Small Ovals
   eight same Small Ovals

APPLIQUÉ 3:
   two same Large Ovals
   eight same Small Ovals
   eight same Small Ovals
   four same Small Ovals

(continued)

Triptych Blueprint

PATCHWORK SEWING

1. For A blocks, use the two-at-a-time method to make ten two-color HSTs and trim to 9½" (24.1 cm).

2. For B blocks, use the two-at-a-time method to make ten two-color HSTs and trim to 9½" (24.1 cm).

3. For C blocks, make twenty Grandmother's Fan Blocks. Save circular appliqué until assembly.

4. For D blocks, make twenty Snowball Blocks; however, only alter two side-by-side corners.

5. For E blocks, sewing the corners is similar to a Snowball corner; however, on one corner there are two sewing steps (pay careful attention to the illustrations) *(Fig. 1)*:

   - On one corner sew the 3" (7.6 cm) square on the angle and trim for a classic Snowball corner.

   - On the next corner sew the 5" (12.7 cm) square on the angle and trim for a Snowball corner.

   - Now on the same corner with the large angle also add the 3" (7.6 cm) square for a second angle.

   - Sew 10 E blocks with the larger double corner at right.

   - Sew 10 E blocks with the larger double corner at left.

APPLIQUÉ AND ASSEMBLY SEWING

The assembly map on page 119 illustrates all the appliqué units and their positions on the quilt.

1. With the A, B, C, and D blocks we will create six-block units in order to create a background on which to perform the repetitive appliqué.

   - Sew block A to block B as shown.

   - Sew two C blocks together as shown.

   - Sew two D blocks together as shown.

   - Assemble the pairs together for the side unit.

2. Repeat step 1 to create a total of ten identical side units. Press well.

3. Appliqué large floral circles over the intersection between A-B-C-C *(Fig. 2)*. Repeat on all ten side units.

4. Fold and press ¼" (6 mm) of long edges of bias arches toward wrong sides. Use curving method to create arches.

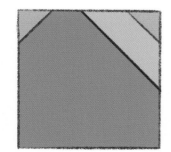

Fig. 1

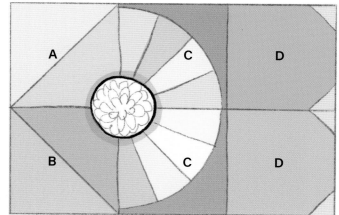

Fig. 2

5. On a side unit, mark with a straight pin 5" (12.7 cm) above the seam between A/B and C on each side as shown in illustration *(Fig. 3)*. This is where you will place the ends of the curved arch on each side. Position the wrong side of the bias into place and press further to achieve the desired curve before pinning or glue tacking into place. Notice the top center of the arches is just above the D block seam.

6. Use your desired appliqué sewing method to sew the arch in place. Repeat arch appliqué on all ten of the side units. Press them well, and trim off any excess bias in line with side unit edges.

7. Position and appliqué four small leaves (dull aqua) on their points along the arch shape. Repeat this appliqué sewing on all ten side units. Press well.

8. You can now assemble both side columns by sewing one side unit to the next for five on each side. Pay careful attention to the arch bias meeting at seams as best you can, easing where necessary. Press these seams open.

9. Position and sew the four-piece appliqué elements (three small leaves, one large) at the seam between the units and where the arches meet in the "dip" of the scallop pattern. Complete all eight appliqué elements on both side columns. Press completed side columns well.

10. Create five units of four E blocks as shown with the large angled corners on the four outer corners of the unit *(Fig. 4)*. These are now center units.

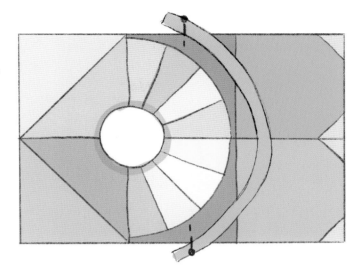

Fig. 3

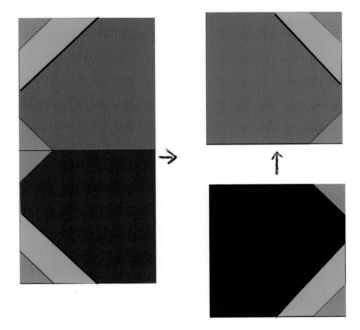

Fig. 4

(continued)

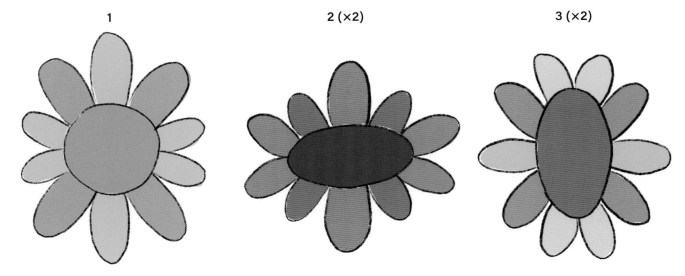

1   2 (×2)   3 (×2)

Fig. 5

11. Position and appliqué the Appliqué 1 design on the center unit that you would like to appear in the center of the quilt *(Fig. 5)*.

12. Position and appliqué the Appliqué 2 design on the center units (two of them) that you would like to be on the top and bottom of the center of the quilt.

13. Position and appliqué the Appliqué 3 design on the center units (two of them) that you would like to be at the very top and bottom of the center column.

14. Once all of these center units have the appliqué completed, you can assemble them one to the next to create the center column of the quilt.

15. Sew the side columns on either side of the center column for the final assembly of the quilt, making sure to match seam intersections and nesting seam allowances as best you can.

16. Press the entire top well before backing, quilting, and binding as desired.

The slow but enjoyable work of the leaf appliqué was well worth the time.

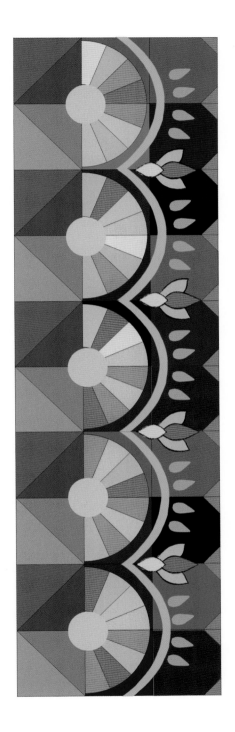

Assembly Map

SAWTOOTH TOTE

As a delightful diversion from the quilts for a moment, we are taking the simplest patchwork inspiration and making an unexpected twist on the basic tote. Staying within our Triptych composition features, the tote panels feature one center panel and two side panels. The small scale Half-Square Triangles in rows and set against either side of the center panel are an eye-catching detail giving the tote its "Sawtooth" name.

COLOR NOTES

I saved this beautiful piece of Japanese linen for a special project where the fabric can do all the heavy lifting. Taking all my color cues from the palette of the floral design, I decided to pair it with a beautiful small-scale print in an almost identical palette and a very simple black print. The black avoids being boring with tiny little white dots. Lining the bag with the small-scale print keeps the whole tote cheery.

....

Size: 26" × 18" (66 × 45.7 cm) (flat)

....

Building Block: Half-Square Triangle

....

Technique: Machine Patchwork

....

Skill Level: Beginner to Confident Beginner

....

FABRICS

⅔ yard (61 cm) feature floral

1½ yards (137.2 cm) small-scale floral

1 yard (91.4 cm) black tonal

1½ yards (137.2 cm) fusible interfacing (I used Pellon® SF101 Shape-Flex®)

thread for machine quilting

four printouts of 1½ HST paper (enough to make seventy-eight)

Optional if quilting the bag:

1¼ yards (114.3 cm) of muslin for backing

approximately 30" × 40" (76.2 × 101.6 cm) of quilt batting

CUTTING

1. Cut two center panels from feature floral fabric measuring 12½" × 18½" (31.8 × 47 cm).

2. Cut four side panels from black tonal fabric measuring 6" × 18½" (15.2 × 47 cm).

*3. Cut four HST pages from black tonal fabric measuring 8½" × 11" (21.6 × 27.9 cm).

*4. Cut four HST pages from small floral fabric measuring 8½" × 11" (21.6 × 27.9 cm).

   Note: If you don't want to use the HST paper, you can create seventy-eight HSTs in your desired method that finish at 1½" (3.8 cm).

5. Cut two lining panels from small floral fabric measuring 26½" × 18½" (67.3 × 47 cm).

   • If quilting the outer panels, then also cut two backing panels 26½" × 18½" (67.3 × 47 cm).

(continued)

6. Cut two strap panels from small floral measuring 2" × 23" (5.1 × 58.4 cm).

7. Cut two interfacing panels measuring 26½" × 18½" (67.3 × 47 cm).

8. Cut two strap interfacing pieces measuring 1½" × 23" (3.8 × 58.4 cm).

SEWING

Note that patchwork sewing uses ¼" (6 mm) seam allowances (to create panels), but tote construction uses ½" (13 mm) seam allowances in some places where noted.

1. To create HSTs using the paper method, place the two fabrics right sides together on the back side of the printed paper and pin at corners. From the right side of the paper, machine stitch along all the solid lines with a small stitch length (yes, through the paper).

2. Once all lines are sewn, cut on the dotted lines. Carefully remove the papers from the sewn HSTs. It might help to fold the paper along the perforated stitch lines and gently tear. While this paper method might seem tedious, it avoids trimming all the HSTs to the final size.

3. Repeat steps 1 and 2 until you have created seventy-eight HSTs and press well.

4. Sew the HSTs into six different rows with the following numbers and press each well:
   - four rows using twelve HSTs
   - two rows using fifteen HSTs

5. Sew a row of twelve HSTs on either side of a center panel *(Fig. 1)*. Repeat with the remaining twelve HST row.

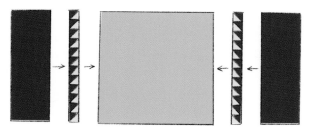

Fig. 1

6. Sew a side panel on either side of the center panel. Repeat with the remaining center panel. These are now outer panels. Press well *(Fig. 1)*.

7. Sew the outer panels right sides together on their bottom seam only using ½" (13 mm) seam allowance. Press open.

QUILTING (optional)

If not quilting, skip ahead to step 8.

- Sew the backing panels together along the bottom edge using ½" (13 mm) seam allowance and press open.
- Create a quilt sandwich by placing batting between the wrong sides of outer panels and backing panels. You can either spray baste them together or use safety pins.
- Machine quilt in your preferred design. I used washi tape to mark out diagonal lines in both directions to achieve a square on point design.
- Press well and trim excess batting away before continuing to step 8.

8. Prepare the lining panels with your preferred interfacing. Sew the lining panels together along the side and bottom edges using ½" (13 mm) seam allowance, but leave an opening of about 6" to 8" (15.2 to 20.3 cm) in the center bottom seam of the lining *(Fig. 2)*. Set aside.

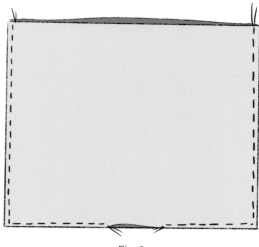

Fig. 2

(continued)

Triptych Blueprint

9. With right sides together, sew outer panels on both side and bottom edges (a U-shape seam) using ½" (13 mm) seam allowance. Press open.

10. Pull outer panels away from each other at one bottom corner and align the right sides of the bottom seam line with the side seam line, then press together, thereby creating a triangular corner. Pin in place. Slide a measuring device across the triangle's base, and keep moving it toward or away from the top triangular point, until you've arrived at a 4" (10.2 cm) distance at the base of the triangle (see illustration for reference). Mark the line, then sew right onto the line to create the box corner. This seam will be perpendicular to the side seams. Begin and end with backstitch, then trim the corner seam allowance off. Repeat at the other side of the tote (Fig. 3).

11. Repeat step 10 to create box corners in the lining of the tote as well.

12. Prepare straps by pressing interfacing onto the wrong side of the straps in the center. Wrap ¼" (6 mm) of the long edges of the pieced strap around the interfacing and tack with glue or pins before pressing to help hold the fold.

13. Fold and press the long edges of the two strap lining pieces ¼" (6 mm) toward the wrong side.

14. Layer the wrong side of the folded strap lining to the wrong side of the folded strap and pin or glue tack to hold together. Now topstitch through all layers with a scant ¼" (6 mm) seam allowance from the folded edges. Complete with both straps and press well.

15. Sew the short ends of one strap to the top edge of one outer panel in a way that continues the Saw-tooth design of the HST design. Make sure not to twist the straps and to sew across a few times for added security. Do this on the remaining outer panel.

16. With right sides together, drop the outer tote into the lining of the tote, align the side seam allowances, and pin in place all around the top edges, keeping the straps dropped down and away from the top edges.

17. Sew all around the top edge of the tote, using a ¼" (6 mm) seam allowance.

18. Turn the bag right side out by pulling the outer bag through the opening in the bottom of the bag lining. Topstitch the opening closed before returning it into the bottom of the inside of the bag.

19. Press the bag well all over, and smooth the upper edge neatly so that the seam between the outer and lining bags is settled at the very top edge. Topstitch this edge all around the top of the bag to stabilize.

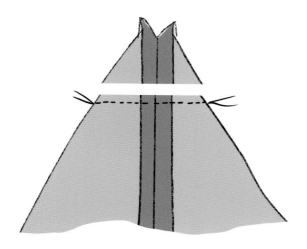

Fig. 3

Anna Maria's Blueprint Quilting

BLUEPRINT

3

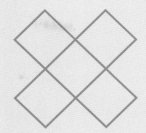

KISS ON THE LIPS

The "X" style format for a quilt has been a longtime favorite of mine ever since I first experimented with the layout in my Cross-Country Quilt from 2016. There is something very contemporary yet nostalgic about this front and center design. You will find the X is more or less obvious as we work our way through four patchwork projects that are all square and made from square blocks set on point.

KALEIDOSCOPE QUILT

I combined two very simple block styles for this quilt and set them on point for added interest. The Snowball and the Shoofly Blocks share the same size corner patch, so the design is very balanced with those little points showing up regularly across the quilt.

COLOR NOTES

At a glance, the color palette seems a bit primary (red, yellow, blue), but there are lovely purples added into the rich blue layers that really help the yellows sing from the center. The × design is very subtle but made apparent with the color changes between the blocks. Part of what makes this quilt beginner friendly is not just the simple patchwork, but also because there are only a total of seven different block styles. This equilateral repetition of shape and color is a foolproof path to success.

....

Size: 64" square (162.6 cm)

....

Block Size: 9" (22.9 cm) finished

....

Building Blocks: Snowball, Shoofly

....

Technique: Machine Patchwork

....

Skill Level: Confident Beginner

....

FABRICS

Note: The following seven block styles (A through G) include details for colors used and amounts of each.

Block A / Shoofly

fat quarter of bright pink (will also be used in Block F)

fat quarter of medium pink

Block B / Snowball

four large red/yellow circular motifs (9½" [24.1 cm] cut size)

fat quarter of bright red

Block C / Shoofly

fat quarter lime green

fat quarter green/gold

fat quarter coral

Block D / Shoofly

fat quarter each of three assorted yellows

Block E / Snowball

eight large blue circular motifs (9½" [24.1 cm] cut size)

thirty-two coral floral elements (3½" [8.9 cm] fussy-cut size)

Block F / Snowball

⅓ yard turquoise floral

(reuse bright pink from block A)

Block G Shoofly

sixteen dark plum flowers (3½" [8.9 cm] fussy-cut size)

¾ yard (68.6 cm) multi purple floral

¾ yard (68.6 cm) aqua tonal

(continued)

YOU WILL ALSO NEED:

1 yard (91.4 cm) of black tonal fabric used throughout

⅓ yard (30.5 cm) of medium blue tonal

1 yard (91.4 cm) of navy/blue geometric print for setting triangles

Batting: 72" × 72" (182.9 × 182.9 cm)

Backing: 4½ yards (4.1 cm)

Binding: 8 yards (7.3 m) of binding

CUTTING

Cutting is organized by block to keep fabrics tidy.

1. For block A, cut:
   - five 3½" (8.9 cm) squares from bright pink fabric
   - four 3½" (8.9 cm) squares from medium pink fabric

2. For blocks B, cut:
   - four 9½" squares from large red/yellow circular motif
   - sixteen 3½" (8.9 cm) squares from bright red fabric

3. For blocks C, cut:
   - four 3½" (8.9 cm) squares from coral fabric
   - sixteen 3½" (8.9 cm) squares from lime green fabric
   - sixteen 3½" (8.9 cm) squares from green/gold fabric

4. For blocks D, cut:
   - four 3½" (8.9 cm) squares from one of the yellow fabrics
   - sixteen 3½" (8.9 cm) squares from the second yellow fabric
   - sixteen 3½" (8.9 cm) squares from the third yellow fabric

5. For blocks E, cut:
   - eight 9½" squares on large blue circular motif
   - thirty-two 3½" (8.9 cm) squares from coral floral motifs

6. For blocks F, cut:
   - four 9½" squares from turquoise floral print
   - sixteen 3½" (8.9 cm) squares from bright pink fabric

7. For blocks G, cut:
   - sixteen 3½" (8.9 cm) squares from dark plum flowers fabric
   - sixty-four 3½" (8.9 cm) squares from multi purple floral print
   - sixty-four 3½" (8.9 cm) squares from aqua tonal print

8. For corners of blocks A, C, D, and G, cut eighty 3½" (8.9 cm) squares from black tonal fabric.

9. For lighter corners of blocks G, cut twenty 3½" (8.9 cm) squares from medium blue tonal.

10. For setting and corner triangles, cut:
    - four 14" (35.6 cm) squares of navy blue geometric (sub-cut each twice on the diagonal for a total of sixteen setting triangles)
    - two 7¼" (18.4 cm) squares of navy blue geometric (sub-cut each once on the angle for a total of four corner triangles)

SEWING

The assembly map on page 133 details the color arrangement for each block as well as the sequence of final assembly. Note that blocks A, C, and D begin as simple 9-Patch Blocks with noted colors before becoming Shoofly Blocks with the addition of black corners.

1. For A, create a 9-Patch Block alternating between the two pink shades. Set aside.

2. For B, create four Snowball Blocks with red fabrics to complete.

3. For C, create four 9-Patch Blocks alternating between lime and green fabrics with coral in the center. Set aside.

4. For D, create four 9-Patch Blocks alternating between two yellow fabrics and the third darker yellow in the center. Set aside.

(continued)

Kiss on the Lips Blueprint

5. For E, create eight Snowball Blocks with blue floral center and coral corners to complete.

6. For F, create four Snowball Blocks with turquoise center and pink corners to complete.

7. For G, create sixteen 9-Patch Blocks alternating between purple and aqua with dark plum in the center. Set aside.

8. With all of blocks A, C, and D, create Snowball corners (which will turn them into Shoofly Blocks) by sewing the 3½" (8.9 cm) squares on the corners and then trim away excess. Press well.

9. With twelve of the G blocks, create Snowball corners by sewing black 3½" (8.9 cm) squares on three of the corners and medium blue 3½" (8.9 cm) on the remaining one corner. Press well. These will go on all side edges of the quilt with blue corners pointing out.

10. With the remaining four G blocks, create Snowball corners by sewing black 3½" (8.9 cm) squares on two of the corners and medium blue 3½" (8.9 cm) on the opposite two corners. Press well. These will go in the four corners of the quilt with blue corners pointing out.

ASSEMBLY

The assembly map shows you the layout with the blocks marked by their letter. The rows will be assembled on the angle.

1. Sew one block to the next in the long diagonal center row. Note that the ends of the center row have the corner triangles from sewing step 10. Sew the long edges of those triangles to each end of the center row. Press all seam allowances in one direction.

2. Sew the rest of the rows in the same manner. Both ends of the remaining rows will have a setting triangle attached; be sure it is oriented the correct way before sewing. Press the subsequent row seam allowances all in the opposite direction of the previous. Continue to alternate seam allowances so that they nest smoothly together in assembly.

3. Once all of the diagonal rows are assembled, begin sewing one row to the next, matching the seam intersections. Pin the rows before sewing if it helps. Continue until the top is assembled.

4. Give the quilt a good pressing before quilting and binding as desired.

Anna Maria's Blueprint Quilting

Assembly Map

BASKET OF FLOWERS QUILT

For this quilt I took one of my favorite blocks, the Dresden Plate, and paired it with some simple geometric 16-Patch Blocks. All the flowers keep your interest by alternating the size of their circular centers. Meanwhile the placement of the Whippersnapper Blocks and Half-Square Triangles wrapping around the corners appear like the turn of a basket handle. And while the appliqué flowers hold our attention in the center, they are balanced by florals in the form of a large-scale print at the outer edges.

COLOR NOTES

The warm yellows and sienna tones of the 16-Patch Blocks emulate a woven basket, while the pinks and purples of the floral blocks highlight the yellow/purple color story. The deep aqua and blue punctuated by black in the center highlights the × shape while keeping the palette more interesting.

....

Size: 85" (215.9 cm) square

....

Block Size: 12" (30.5 cm) finished

....

Building Blocks: Flower, Dresden Plate, 16-Patch, Whippersnapper, Half-Square Triangle

....

Templates Used: Large Circle, Small Circle, Medium Petal, Short Petal

....

Techniques: Machine Patchwork and Appliqué

....

Skill Level: Intermediate

....

FABRICS

Note: The following eight block styles (A through H) include details for colors used and amounts of each.

Block A / Dresden Plate (large center)

large yellow floral for center

fat quarter of feature green

fat quarter of feature coral

fat quarter of deep aqua

Block B / Dresden Plate (large center)

fat quarter of hot pink floral for centers

¼ yard (22.9 cm) of pale blue geometric

¼ yard (22.9 cm) of plum

¾ yard (68.6 cm) of deep aqua (different than A)

Block C / Dresden Plate (small center)

scrap of bright aqua for centers

¼ yard (22.9 cm) of bright yellow

¼ yard (22.9 cm) of coral

¾ yard (68.6 cm) of black

Block D / 16-Patch

⅔ yard (61 cm) of bright orange/yellow

⅔ yard (61 cm) of caramel/brown

Block E / 16-Patch

⅔ yard (61 cm) of lighter gold tonal

⅔ yard (61 cm) of darker gold tonal

Block F / Whippersnapper

½ yard (45.7 cm) of dark blue stripes

scraps of plums and magentas for strip piecing

scraps of pale pinks and lavender for strip piecing

(continued)

Block G / Half-Square Triangle

1 yard (91.4 cm) of plum (will also use for H)

½ yard (45.7 cm) of pale lavender

Block H / Half-Square Triangle

leftover plum from G

½ yard (45.7 cm) of bright pink

YOU WILL ALSO NEED:

1½ yards (137.2 cm) of large lavender and pink floral fabric for large and small setting triangles.

CUTTING

Cutting is organized by block to keep fabrics in order.

1. For block A, cut:
    - (fussy-cut) one Large Circle from yellow floral
    - six Short Petals from feature green fabric
    - six Short Petals from feature coral fabric
    - One 12½" (31.8 cm) square from deep aqua fabric

2. For blocks B, cut:
    - four Large Circles from hot pink floral
    - twenty-four Short Petals from pale blue geometric
    - twenty-four Short Petals from plum print
    - four 12½" (31.8 cm) squares from deep aqua fabric

3. For blocks C, cut:
    - (fussy-cut) four Small Circles from bright aqua print
    - twenty-four Medium Petals from bright yellow geometric
    - twenty-four Medium Petals from coral geometric
    - four 12½" (31.8 cm) squares from black print

4. For blocks D, cut:
    - six 3½" (8.9 cm) wide × WOF strips from bright orange/yellow print
    - six 3½" (8.9 cm) wide × WOF strips from caramel/brown print

5. For blocks E, cut:
    - six 3½" (8.9 cm) wide × WOF strips from lighter gold print
    - six 3½" (8.9 cm) wide × WOF strips from darker gold print

6. For blocks F, cut:
    - one 13½" (34.3 cm) square from dark blue stripe, then sub-cut on both angles to create four triangles
    - various widths (1½" to 2½" [3.8 to 6.4 cm]) and lengths (6" to 18" [15.2 to 45.7 cm]) from plum and magenta scraps
    - various widths (1½" to 2½" [3.8 to 6.4 cm]) and lengths (6" to 18" [15.2 to 45.7 cm]) from pale pink and lavender scraps

7. For blocks G, cut:
    - four 13½" (34.3 cm) squares from plum print (reserve two for H)
    - two 13½" (34.3 cm) squares from pale lavender

8. For blocks H, cut:
    - (two plum print squares from previous step)
    - two 13½" (34.3 cm) squares from bright pink print

9. For large setting triangles, cut:
    - two 26" (66 cm) triangles from large lavender and pink floral (sub-cut each square on the diagonal for a total of four triangles)

10. For smaller setting triangles, cut:
    - four 13½" (34.3 cm) squares from large lavender and pink floral (sub-cut each square on the diagonal once for a total of eight triangles)

(continued)

Kiss on the Lips Blueprint

SEWING

1. For A, use your desired appliqué method to create one Dresden Plate Block by alternating the two different colors of Short Petals in assembly.

2. For B, use your desired appliqué method to create four Dresden Plate Blocks by alternating the two different colors of Short Petals in assembly.

3. For C, use your desired appliqué method to create four Dresden Plate Blocks by alternating the two different colors of Medium Petals in assembly.

4. For D, use the alternating strip piecing method to create eight 16-Patch Blocks.

5. For E, use the alternating strip piecing method to create eight 16-Patch Blocks.

6. For F, using the dark blue triangles as a base, begin building the plum and magenta scraps as the short strips to the right side. Use the pale pink and lavender as the long strips and build them to the left side to create four Whippersnapper Blocks. Trim to 12½" (31.8 cm) when complete.

7. For G, using the two-at-a-time method, create four HSTs from the plum and pale lavender that are trimmed to 12½" (31.8 cm) when complete.

8. For H, using the two-at-a-time method, create four HSTs from the plum and bright pink that are trimmed to 12½" (31.8 cm) when complete.

ASSEMBLY

The assembly map shows you the layout with the blocks marked by their letter. The rows will be assembled on the angle.

1. Sew one block to the next in the long center row. Note that the center row has the Whippersnapper Blocks at each end. Press seam allowances in one direction.

2. Sew the next rows that are adjacent to the center row (in either direction) one block to the next. Press the seam allowances of these rows in the opposite direction of the center row.

3. Assemble these three rows together, nesting their seam allowances in opposite directions as their block seams intersect. Press well.

4. Now sew the longest edge of a large setting triangle to both ends of the set of three rows. Press away from the center.

5. Continue building out from the center to sew together subsequent rows as shown, alternating the direction of how you press the seam allowances. These rows will begin and end with the smaller setting triangles, so make sure you have those oriented the correct way.

6. Once the remaining four rows are assembled, you can assemble the units on either side of the center before joining each of them to the remaining two large setting triangles.

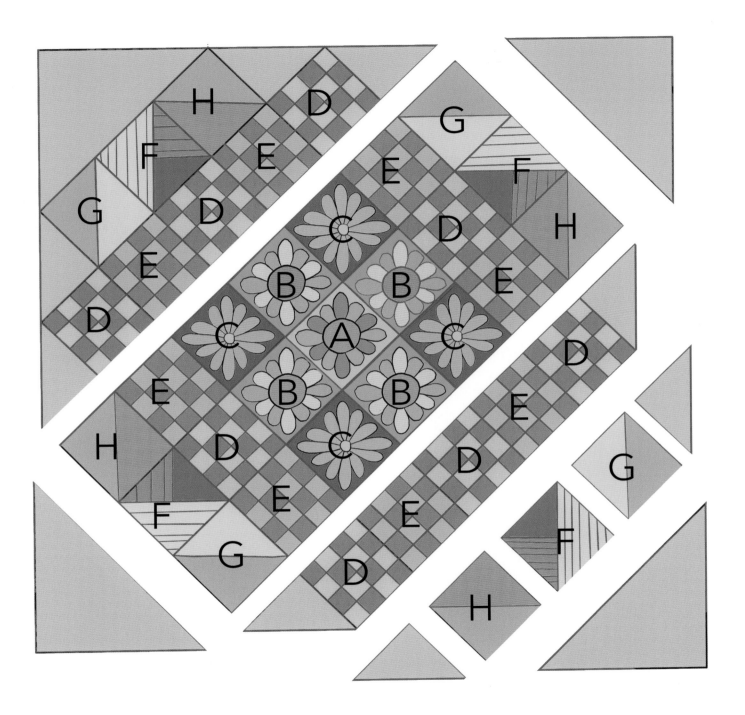

Assembly Map

OPEN BORDERS QUILT

This quilt is very special to me because it was made while I was waiting for the world and travel to open up again during the pandemic. Based on the benign 12" (30.5 cm) block, the regular arrangement of elements through radial symmetry really helps corral all of the color and pattern into something pleasing to the eye. There is also a healthy amount of variation in the piece sizes of the patchwork so that it is interesting despite the regular block size. I can assure you that it is simply the combination of these elements that makes the quilt appear trickier than it is to assemble. But like most beautiful endeavors, it will not be quick.

COLOR NOTES

This is one of those quilts where more is more. It has all the charm and variation of a scrap quilt but with the organization of something more contemporary. Because there is so much color in the palette, the most important thing is to include some earthy tones alongside the bright ones. The light in the center and the dark toward the edges really helps draw your eye in and hold everything in a suspended glow that avoids chaos.

Size: 85" (215.9 cm) square

Block Size: 12" (30.5 cm) finished

Building Blocks: Log Cabin, Half-Square Triangle, Light Ray

Templates: Small Swoop, Large Swoop, Large Leaf, Medium Petal, Small Oval, Large Oval, Light Ray A and B

Techniques: Machine Patchwork and Appliqué

Skill Level: Intermediate to Advanced

FABRICS

Note: The following nine block styles (A through I) include details for colors used in the patchwork and the yardage estimates for each. Also, these requirements are followed by more general fabric indications used in the appliqué features.

Block A / Log Cabin

scraps of bright and pale colored fabrics

Block B / Whole Square

¾ yard (68.6 cm) of pale floral

Block C / Light Ray

½ yard (45.7 cm) each of pink tonal, multifloral, green tonal, and coral

Block D / Whole Square

1¼ yards (114.3 cm) of multicolored plaid

(continued)

Block E / Half-Square Triangle (and corner triangles)

½ yard (45.7 cm) of blue stripe

⅔ yard (61 cm) of dark green stripe

Block F / Light Ray

½ yard (45.7 cm) each of green/blue, black/brown, black multifloral, and purple

Block G / custom patchwork

½ yard (45.7 cm) each of bright yellow and blue

¾ yard (68.6 cm) each of lavender and yellow floral

Block H / Log Cabin

fat quarter each of thirteen different deep and earthy fabrics

Block I / 36-patch

quarter yards or scraps of at least twelve different small-scale print fabrics that have a broad range of color and value

APPLIQUÉ:

Five-piece appliqué units on corners of block A:

fat quarters of lavender/gold/blue

Fan flower units on long leafy stems from each corner:

fat quarter each of six different brightly colored florals (mostly light, also a couple darker)

⅔ yard (61 cm) of blue-green floral

⅔ yard (61 cm) of coral/red floral

⅔ yard (61 cm) of rich brown

⅓ yard (30.5 cm) of black tonal

Four large blue floral elements for E blocks

YOU WILL ALSO NEED:

Batting: 90" × 90" (228.6 × 228.6 cm)

Backing: 5½ yards (5 m)

Binding: 10½ yards (9.6 m)

PATCHWORK CUTTING

Cutting is organized by block to keep fabrics tidy.

1. For block A, cut the following Log Cabin pieces from various bright and pale scraps:
   - 3½" (8.9 cm) square
   - 2" × 3½" (5.1 × 8.9 cm) rectangle
   - two different 2" × 5" (5.1 × 12.7 cm) rectangles
   - two different 2" × 6½" (5.1 × 16.5 cm) rectangles
   - two different 2" × 8" (5.1 × 20.3 cm) rectangles
   - two different 2" × 9½" (5.1 × 24.1 cm) rectangles
   - two different 2" × 11" (5.1 × 27.9 cm) rectangles
   - one 2" × 12½" (5.1 × 31.8 cm) rectangle

2. For blocks B, cut four 12½" (31.8 cm) squares.

3. For blocks C, use Light Ray Block templates A and B to cut the following:
   - Layer coral and pink fabric right sides together and cut using template A so that the two resulting pieces are mirror images of each other. Repeat three more times for a total of eight pieces.
   - Layer green tonal and multifloral fabrics right sides together and cut using template B so that the two resulting pieces are mirror images of each other. Repeat three more times for a total of eight pieces.

4. For blocks D, cut eight 12½" (31.8 cm) squares.

5. For blocks E, cut two 13½" (34.3 cm) squares each from green stripe and blue stripe.

6. Blocks F:

   Note that for these eight Light Ray Blocks, four are colored one way, and the other four are colored in a mirror direction, so the cutting is not like blocks C. Fold each of the four colors of fabric against themselves, right sides together, and cut two at a time:
   - template A from purple print for a total of eight pieces
   - template A from green/blue print for a total of eight pieces
   - template B from black/brown print for a total of eight pieces
   - template B from black multifloral for a total of eight pieces

(continued)

Kiss on the Lips Blueprint

7. For blocks G, (which finish at 12" × 24" [30.5 × 61 cm]), cut:
    - four 6½" × 12½" (16.5 × 31.8 cm) rectangles from bright yellow print
    - four 6½" × 12½" (16.5 × 31.8 cm) rectangles from bright blue print
    - four 12½" × 12½" (31.8 × 31.8 cm) rectangles from lavender and yellow floral

8. For block H, cut the following Log Cabin pieces from various fat quarters of deep and earthy fabrics (cut each piece from the same fabric four times so that you can make four of the same block):
    - 3½" (8.9 cm) square
    - 2" × 3½" (5.1 × 8.9 cm) rectangle
    - two different 2" × 5" (5.1 × 12.7 cm) rectangles
    - two different 2" × 6½" (5.1 × 16.5 cm) rectangles
    - two different 2" × 8" (5.1 × 20.3 cm) rectangles
    - two different 2" × 9½" (5.1 × 24.1 cm) rectangles
    - two different 2" × 11" (5.1 × 27.9 cm) rectangles
    - one 2" × 12½" (5.1 × 31.8 cm) rectangle

9. For Block I, cut 2½" (6.4 cm) × WOF strips of the various small prints. Whether you made every patchwork setting triangle identical from the placement of same fabrics or you don't plan the style of scraps, you will need to sub-cut twenty-one 2½" (6.4 cm) squares from the strips for each of the sixteen blocks (336 total).

10. For corner setting triangles, cut two 8½" (21.6 cm) squares from dark green stripe fabric, then sub-cut each on the diagonal to yield four triangles.

APPLIQUÉ CUTTING

1. For the four five-piece appliqué units on the corners of Block A, cut:
    - four Medium Petals from blue
    - eight Large Leaves from gold
    - eight Small Swoops from lavender

2. For long leafy fan flowers from each quilt corner, cut:
    - four Medium Petals of a dark color
    - eight Medium Petals of each of three other bright colors
    - four Large Ovals of a fourth bright color
    - four Small Ovals of a dark color
    - sixteen Small Swoops from blue-green (eight right facing, eight left facing)
    - sixteen Large Swoops from blue-green (eight right facing, eight left facing)
    - eight Small Swoops from coral/red (four right facing, four left facing)
    - twenty-four Large Swoops from coral/red (twelve right facing, twelve left facing)
    - four 1½" × 36" (3.8 × 91.4 cm) bias lengths of rich brown print
    - four 1½" × 24½" (3.8 × 62.2 cm) lengths of black tonal print

3. For E blocks, cut four large blue flowers organically around the shape of the floral element (leaving seam allowance or not depending on your chosen appliqué method).

SEWING

The assembly map on page 149 will help note the style and color of blocks.

1. For A, sew a Log Cabin Block with all of the A pieces. Press well.

2. For B, gather the four background squares, the Medium Petals for fan flowers, and decide on an arrangement of seven petals for each block. Prepare appliqué pieces for sewing, keep pieces grouped together, and set aside.

3. For C, sew four identical Ray Blocks using one piece of each color. Press well.

4. For D, sort all of the whole square blocks and prep 16 Small Swoop and 16 Large Swoop blue-green appliqué pieces for appliqué and set aside.

5. For E, use the two-at-a-time method to create four Half-Square Triangles. Use any appliqué method desired to sew the large-scale blue flower onto the HSTs. I chose to center my flower more over on the dark green side of the HST, but you can arrange however you feel is most pleasing. Arrange and sew all four blocks the same way. Press well.

6. For F, sew all eight Ray Blocks. As noted in the cutting instructions, make sure that the color and fabric arrangement in four of the blocks mirrors the arrangement in the other four blocks. Press well.

7. For G, sew the bright yellow rectangles at one side of the lavender floral square, and sew the bright blue rectangle at the opposite side of the square. Repeat this for all four G blocks and press well. Gather all of the stems (brown and black) as well as the coral/red swoops and prepare all of the pieces for appliqué. Group each set of four shapes together with the G blocks and set aside.

8. For H, sew four Log Cabin Blocks using all of the pieces cut for H blocks. Make sure they are identical.

9. For I, arrange and sew setting triangles with twenty-one squares in the formation of a triangle in your desired arrangement. I made an attempt to use the darker fabrics at the center point of the right triangle and they gradually got lighter as they passed toward what will become the outer edges of the quilt. I also chose to make all my triangular blocks identical in their fabric arrangement. Complete sixteen setting triangles and press well. (The irregular edge of these blocks will be trimmed in the final step of assembly.)

(continued)

ASSEMBLY

Note that the assembly steps include all of the appliqué sewing as most of these pieces are sewn over the top of joined blocks; therefore, a certain sequence is required. Although you can sew the entire quilt top together before performing the appliqué, that leaves you with a very large background to manage the sewing of many smaller pieces. Therefore, the sequence that I am offering generally allows you to perform appliqué on smaller backgrounds as you go. If you feel a different sequence would suit your process better, you can absolutely make changes to the process. The assembly map on page 149 does not show an order of assembly sewing but rather the relative position of each block and appliqué unit. Make sure to alternate pressing between blocks and rows to nest seam allowances and avoid bulk as you go.

1. Sew two B blocks to opposite sides of the A block.

2. Sew one B block in between two C blocks, making sure that the narrow points of the C blocks are both at the same end of B. Repeat to create a duplicate unit of three with remaining B and C blocks.

3. Assemble the three units of three created in steps 1 and 2 to create the center 9-Patch of the quilt *(Fig. 1)*.

4. You can now perform the appliqué of the five-piece petal, leaf, and swoop units as shown at the four corners of the A block and centered over the C blocks. (Keep in mind all of the sewing with these units is appliqué, and simply layered one over the other create symmetry *[Fig. 2]*. There are no actual seams between pieces.) Press well and set aside.

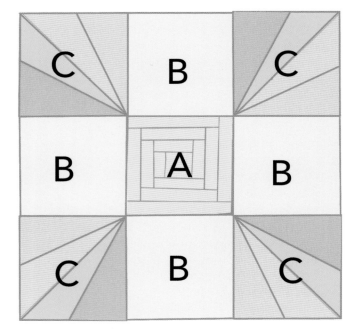

Fig. 1

Fig. 2

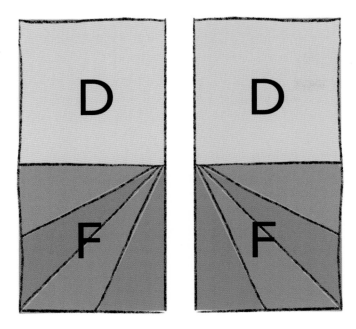

Fig. 3

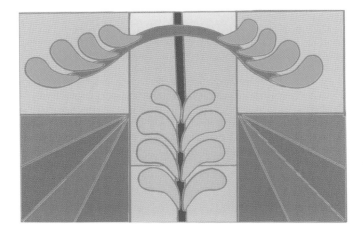

Fig. 4

5. Pair together all D and F blocks. Note that in my quilt, I always joined the purple/magenta edge of the F block to the D block when I sewed them together. And if you have correctly mirrored half of the F blocks in their color arrangement to the other half, you will end up with eight mirrored D/F pairs as shown as well. Sew all D/F pairs and press well *(Fig. 3)*.

6. Appliqué the straight black stems onto the G blocks, centered lengthwise. Also appliqué two small and six large coral red swoops along either side of the stem. Note that the lowest pair of large swoops is just below the top seam of the bright blue rectangle. The smallest pair of swoops at the top of the swoops is just above the midpoint of the lavender floral square. Repeat and continue this arrangement and appliqué sewing for all four G blocks and press well *(Fig. 4)*.

7. Sew two D/F pairs to both sides of a G block, making sure that the D end of the pair is aligned with the bright yellow end of the G block and the blue-green edge of the F block is aligned with the bright blue end of the G block. (See illustration.) Repeat sewing this unit for a total of four D/F/G units.

8. You can now appliqué the curved brown stems and blue-green swoops across the D/G/D blocks of the units made in the previous step. (Use the bias curving techniques taught in Appliqué Adventures [page 54]. Once you have curved one stem, curve the remaining three stems in the same way so they look uniform.) I kept the center part of the brown stem relatively straight as it passed over the black stem and pretty centered on the bright yellow rectangle. The curving down on each side passes near and just above the seam between the bright yellow and lavender floral. Trimming the length of this stem might be desired depending on your curve and layout. Complete stem and swoop appliqué on all D/F/G units and press well *(Fig. 4)*.

(continued)

9. Arrange and sew together the four identical seven-piece fan flowers (similar to Dresden Plate sewing) to each other and press well. Don't worry if their narrow ends are not perfectly aligned, these will be covered by the oval shapes of appliqué. Complete all four of these appliqué units and press well.

    A note about preparing joined pieces for raw-edge appliqué. As presented in Appliqué Adventures (page 54), you can choose to keep seam allowances on the shapes if you would like to turn them back for needle-turn appliqué. Or you can eliminate seam allowances and use a fusible product to secure raw edges. In this scenario, where we needed to keep the seam allowances in place in order to sew them to each other, you can still choose to use raw edges after the petals are assembled. To do this, press the fusible product onto the back side of the joined set of seven Medium Petals, and then trim away the seam allowance from the curved edges as desired before fusing to background appliqué sewing.

10. You can now sew a D/F/G unit to one side of the A/B/C unit, making sure the bright yellow end of G is against the B block. Press well.

11. Layer one of the seven-piece fan flower units onto the top of the black stem and centered at the outer edge of the B block. The large bright oval will layer onto the intersection of the stems and underneath the fan flower (you can cut away hidden excess). Finally, the small oval will layer atop the large oval and just cover the narrow ends of the fan flower. Secure these shapes and complete the appliqué sewing. Press well.

12. Repeat steps 10 and 11 with another D/F/G unit on the opposite side of the center A/B/C 9-Patch and press well. This is now the quilt center.

13. Sew two I blocks to the dark green edges of an E block and press well. The resulting shape will be a large triangle. Repeat this with the remaining three E blocks and six more I blocks. These are now E/I units.

14. Sew two I blocks to opposite edges of an H block and press well. Repeat this with the remaining three H blocks and remaining six I blocks, making sure all four units look the same. Now sew the long edges of the corner triangles to the same side of all H blocks and press well. These four units are now the quilt corners.

15. Sew the long edge of a quilt corner to two opposite ends of the quilt center and press well.

16. Sew a E/I unit to either side of a D/F/G unit making sure the blue stripe of the E block is aligned with the D blocks. (See quilt photo.) Press well and repeat with the remaining two E/I units and remaining D/F/G unit. These are now the quilt sides.

17. Sew the long edge of a quilt corner to the F block edge of a quilt side. Repeat with the remaining quilt corner and the remaining quilt side and press well.

18. For final assembly, sew the quilt sides to either long edge of the quilt center taking care to align all seam intersections. Press quilt top well.

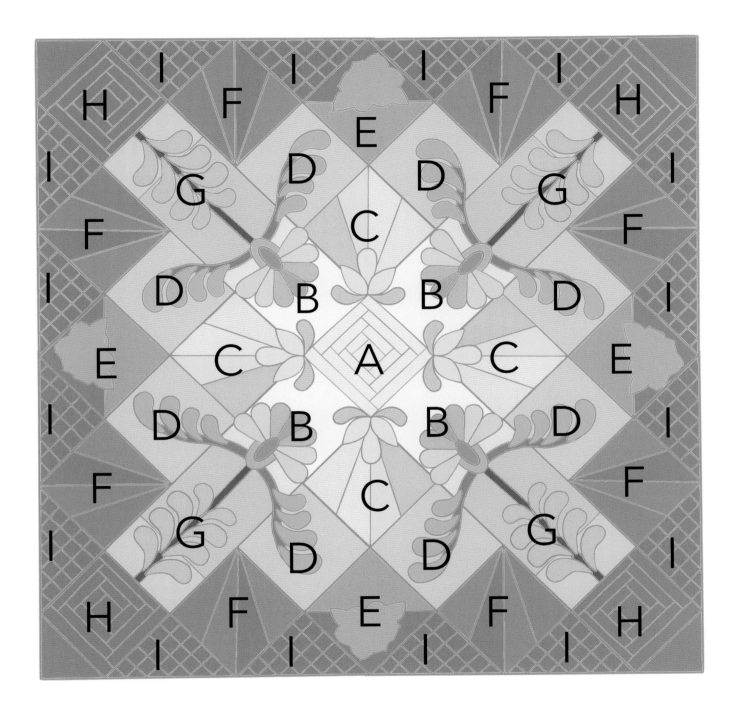

Assembly Map

RISE AND SHINE BABY QUILT

I took a very simple approach to following the "X" in this final Kiss on the Lips Blueprint project. While all of the blocks are the same size, a single floral square on point in the center of the quilt calls attention to itself as it stretches out in four directions (not unlike a waking newborn baby). While the × is visible through the color changes to each of the four corners, the additional color group acts as a framing element to offer a secondary design.

COLOR NOTES

I will admit to indulging in some of my favorite berry, coral, and sunny yellow shades, with lavender and blue accents. However, rather than going full-on print, I played with the palette using multiple solid shades in a paler as well as a deeper assortment. This change in value really organizes the framing features, but the random change in solid color keeps it interesting.

....
Size: 44" (111.8 cm) square
....
Block Size: 5" (12.7 cm) finished
....
Building Blocks: Square, Half-Square Triangle, Quarter-Square Triangle
....
Technique: Machine Patchwork
....
Skill Level: Confident Beginner
....

FABRICS

Solid Fabrics:

Fat quarter each of six assorted shades of deep warm tones (e.g., magenta, purple, burgundy)

Fat quarter each of four assorted shades of pale warm tones (e.g., pink, coral, lavender)

Printed Fabrics:

Note: The following amounts are what I used, but fussy cutting and repeat size affects yardage.

A	Feature center, enough for one 5½" (14 cm) fussy-cut square on point
B	Fat quarter of deep blue/lavender that is good for fussy cutting
C	⅜ yard (34.3 cm) of deep coral floral that is good for fussy cutting
D	Fat quarter bright coral tonal
E	Fat quarter of pink/coral
F	Fat quarter of light blue/lavender
G	Fat quarter of small-scale lavender
H	Fat quarter of hot pink tonal
I	Fat quarter of gold/pink tonal
J	Fat quarter of small-scale aqua/green
K	Fat quarter of bright yellow tonal
L	Fat quarter of gold yellow/aqua
M	Fat quarter of deep multi/royal blue

(continued)

CUTTING

Note that you may cut a few more solids than you need to create all the necessary blocks; however, this will give you some opportunity to be picky about combos.

1. For whole squares, cut 5½" (14 cm) squares in the following quantities from the following fabrics:
   - one from fabric A
   - four from fabric B

2. For Half-Square Triangles, cut 6" (15.2 cm) squares in the following quantities from the following fabrics:
   - two from fabric C (fussy cut if desired)
   - two from fabric E
   - four from fabric F
   - six from fabric K
   - eight from fabric L

3. For Half-Square Triangles and setting triangles, cut 6" (15.2 cm) squares in the following quantities from the following solid fabrics:
   - ten to twelve squares from assorted pale solids
   - eighteen to twenty squares from assorted deep solids

4. For Quarter-Square Triangles, cut 6½" (16.5 cm) squares in the following quantities from the following fabrics:
   - two from fabric D
   - two from fabric E
   - two from fabric G
   - two from fabric H
   - two from fabric J
   - two from fabric L
   - two from fabric C
   - two from fabric M

SEWING

HALF-SQUARE TRIANGLES (HST)

Refer to "Half-Square Triangle" (page 40) for block sewing techniques.

1. Create four HSTs by pairing fabric C with E *(Fig. 1)*.

2. Create eight HSTs by pairing assorted pale solids with fabric F.

3. Create twelve HSTs by pairing assorted pale solids with fabric K.

4. Create sixteen HSTs by pairing assorted deep solids with fabric L.

5. Press and trim all of the HSTs to be 5½" (14 cm) square.

QUARTER-SQUARE TRIANGLE (QST)

Refer to "Quarter-Square Triangle" (page 41) for block sewing techniques.

1. Create four QSTs by pairing fabric D with E *(Fig. 2)*.

2. Create four QSTs by pairing fabric G with H.

3. Create four QSTs by pairing fabric I with J.

4. Create four QSTs by pairing fabric M with C.

5. Press and trim all of the QSTs to be 5½" (14 cm) square.

Fig. 1   Fig. 2

(continued)

Kiss on the Lips Blueprint

ASSEMBLY

1.   Cut all of the remaining deep solid 6" (15.2 cm) squares from one corner to the opposite to create setting triangles. You will need a total of twenty, so cut more 6" (15.2 cm) squares if necessary.

2.   Cut one 6" (15.2 cm) square from the bright coral tonal fabric D, then sub cut from one corner to the opposite, and then do the same in the other direction so that you end up with four triangles. This will be the corner triangles of the quilt.

3.   The assembly map shows you the block layout with the fabric colors marked with their corresponding letters. The pale solids have a * symbol and the deep solids have a = symbol. Use these details to lay out your blocks. As you're laying out the quilt, you can swap some blocks with each other in order to randomize the solids placement. Just be sure that the pale, yellow, and deep solid color borders stay in position.

4.   Sew one block to the next in the long diagonal center row. Note that the end of the center rows has the small triangles attached from step 2. Sew the long edges of those triangles to each end of the center row. Press all seam allowances in one direction.

5.   Sew the rest of the rows in the same manner. Both ends of the remaining rows will have a deep solid setting triangle attached; be sure it is oriented the correct way before sewing. Press the subsequent row seam allowances all in the opposite direction of the first, and continue to alternate seam allowances so that they nest smoothly together in assembly.

6.   Once all of the diagonal rows are assembled, begin sewing one row to the next, matching the seam intersections. Pin the rows before sewing if it helps. Continue until the top is assembled.

7.   Give the quilt a good pressing before quilting and binding as desired.

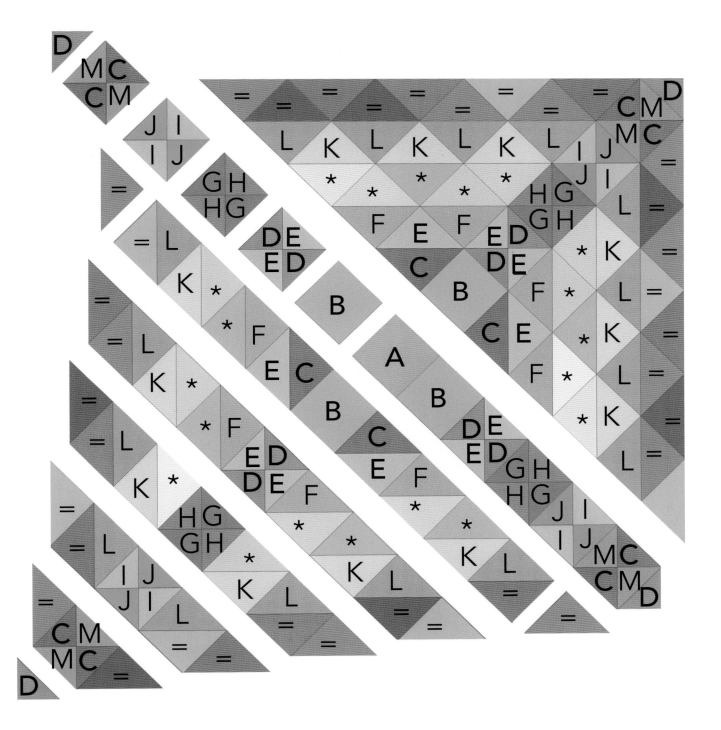

Assembly Map

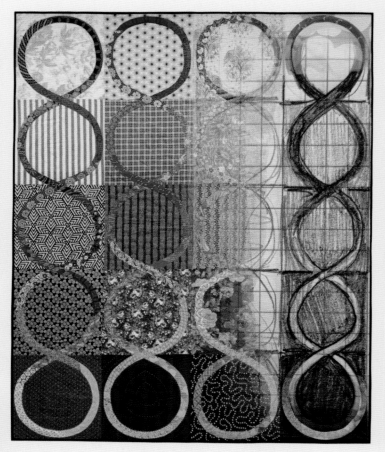

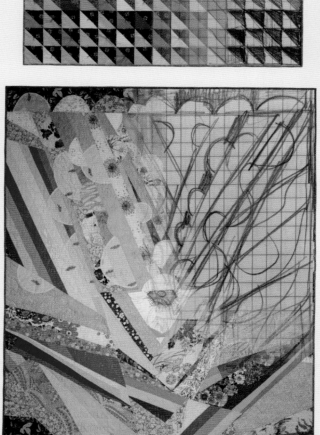

COLOR STUDY

Maybe you didn't see this coming, but it's now time to break my own rules with composition and abandon a specific structure. Or rather, the structure that we are going to follow is somewhat of a moving target. And that structure is *color itself*. These projects are perfect for those quilters who like to feel their way through a project more gently than rigidly. Using color as your guide does not mean that there is no plan, but rather that these color-based pathways can land us in unexpected but very joyful places.

DIP DYED QUILT

I have made several Color Study–type quilts over the years that use the humble Half-Square Triangle. However, I am usually positioning the angles for a secondary design to appear or for the blocks to come together to build a larger shape. For this Dip Dyed Quilt, I really stripped down the ulterior motives to focus on color in a more straightforward approach, and I was excited to see what would happen that I could not plan for.

Size: 60" × 72" (152.4 × 182.9 cm)

Block Size: 4" (10.2 cm) finished

Building Block: Half-Square Triangle

Technique: Machine Patchwork

Skill Level: Beginner

COLOR NOTES

This quilt actually studies color transitions in a few different ways. I assigned half of every HST with a solid fabric and the other half with a printed fabric. While a large majority of those solid/printed pairs celebrate the blue/orange color story in the center of the quilt, each fabric category passes through a few changes from top to bottom. The solid fabrics begin as pinks and reds, go through their orange phase, and finally land as acidic greens and yellows at the bottom edge of the quilt. Meanwhile the printed fabrics, while mostly tonal, begin as pale lime green at the top and pass through various shades of aqua and blue before they finish as a deep, almost black indigo print at the bottom edge. The solids are used more sporadically as they transition from top to bottom, and the prints each are assigned exactly three rows.

FABRICS

Please feel free to create your own color logic for this project using your favorite colors rather than mine, if desired. In addition to using different colors, you can use more or less variety in the sold and print categories to suit your design. The following details what I used:

½ yard (45.7 cm) each of twenty-four different solid fabrics ranging from pink to lime

1 yard (91.4 cm) each of six different printed fabrics ranging from pale lime to indigo

(continued)

BONUS EIGHT-AT-A-TIME HST METHOD

While everything is a finished 4" (10.2 cm) HST, there are six main sections of the quilt marked by the use of the same printed fabric. Every two sections together, however, use mostly the same group of six solids. (Here and there you can see I have used a solid fabric in multiple sections.) You can see this if you look at the main photo of the quilt and the solids used in every two print sections. Because of this, you have the opportunity to make a lot of the same exact HST combos, so using the two-at-a-time method might not suit you. Here are the steps to making eight of the same HST at a time:

1. Cut one 10¼" (26 cm) square from solid and one from print.

2. Layer right sides together and draw diagonal lines two ways from corner to corner.

3. Sew ¼" (6 mm) to the left and right of both of these lines.

4. Cut on the drawn lines.

5. Also cut on the middle of each resulting triangle as shown *(Fig. 1)*.

If you decide to use the eight-at-a-time method here and there, go ahead and cut some of the solids and prints that you want to make a lot of in the 10¼" (26 cm) squares. You will most likely also do some with the two-at-a-time method as well to increase variety. The following cutting instructions follow the two-at-a-time method for the whole quilt.

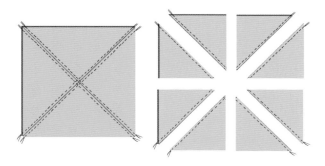

Fig. 1

CUTTING

1. Cut twenty-three 5" (12.7 cm) squares from each of the six printed fabrics.

2. Cut eight 5" (12.7 cm) squares from each of the eighteen solid fabrics.

SEWING & ASSEMBLY

Note that I refer to the six different sections (three rows that use the same print) as sections A, B, C, D, E, and F from the top down.

1. Sew forty-five HSTs using the same print and six different solids for section A.

2. Sew forty-five HSTs using the next print but the same six solids for section B.

3. Repeat steps 1 and 2 with the next two prints and a new set of six solids to make sections C and D.

4. Repeat steps 1 and 2 with the next two prints and a new set of six solids to make sections E and F.

Note that you might want to create a few HSTs that borrow solids from a previous or following section just to dapple the color around here and there as you like. You can move on to assembly once you have 270 (or more) HSTs finished and trimmed to 4½" (11.4 cm) and pressed well.

5. Lay out each color section with three rows high and eighteen blocks wide of the same print and various solids. Once you're pleased with the arrangement, sew one block to the next to form the long horizontal rows. Then assemble the rows to complete section A, alternating seam direction.

6. Repeat step 5 for the remaining sections B through F. Press all sections well.

7. Sew all six sections together in order to complete your quilt top.

8. Give the quilt top a final pressing before backing, quilting, and binding as desired.

Color Study Blueprint

TIME TRAVEL QUILT

This is one of those quilt designs that I must have loosely sketched a few dozen times before I settled on a design. Originally, I had planned a more complex background patchwork and sections of loops that interlocked with each other. I drew, drew, and drew, but each attempt felt tangled. And nothing was really striking me until I decided to pare down the details and do something more straightforward with a very regular block background. What almost felt too simple on paper was a treat to choose fabrics for and so pleasant to slowly needle-turn appliqué.

COLOR NOTES

This might have been the most enjoyable project in the entire book for which to choose fabrics. Once I had settled on a tonal black and white scheme for the background that changes value from top to bottom, it was an eye-opening experience to sort my studio's neutral fabrics and see which values I needed to shop for (fun!). I did have all sorts of options for choosing fabrics for the brightly colored bias loops. Each of the four-color categories experience light, medium, and dark versions as well as some variety in hue and print style. The two warmer vertical loops are bordered by the cooler purple and blue on the right and left edges. The value change in the loops goes in the opposite direction to the value change in the background. This creates a bit of mystery in the center of the quilt where all the medium values reside and a bit more drama where you have dark against light at the top and light against dark at the bottom.

Size: 64" × 80" (162.6 × 203.2 cm)

Block Size: 16" (40.6 cm) finished

Techniques: Machine Patchwork and Appliqué

Skill Level: Intermediate

FABRICS

This is a fat-quarter friendly quilt! Take your time and enjoy this selection process. You may set aside some colors once you see them against the background choices. Also, do not worry if some of your neutral backgrounds are warmer and more yellowish while others are cooler and more purplish. Just focus on arranging them for balance once it's time to assemble the background.

Twenty fat quarters (or half yards) of black/gray/white prints in the following values:

four light

four medium-light

four medium

four medium-dark

four dark

Fifteen to eighteen fat quarters (or scraps) of light to dark prints in each of the following categories:

blue/aqua/green

yellow/gold/brown

pink/coral/magenta

lavender/plum/purple

(continued)

CUTTING

1. For background, cut one 16½" (41.9 cm) square from each neutral fabric for a total of twenty squares.

2. Cut 1¾" (4.4 cm)-wide bias strips of various lengths (no shorter than 6" [15.2 cm] and no longer than 18" [45.7 cm]) from all of your colorful scraps. You may want to take each color category and measure them out to be sure you have roughly 5 yards (4.6 m) of combined length.

SEWING & ASSEMBLY

1. For background, organize the fabrics into the four columns of five blocks that go from top to bottom, starting with the lightest and ending with the darkest. For now, we're only sewing the vertical columns. Sew one block to the next from top to bottom. Press well.

2. For each of the four color categories of bias strips, we will be building a long snake of join bias strip scraps. Organize each color category so that the darkest is in the center, and then they grow toward medium and then lighter in both directions until they have the lightest fabrics on each end. Once the order is determined, sew the strips in this light-med-dark-med-light order by joining them at a 45-degree angle, one to the next as shown *(Fig. 1)*. Trim excess from each seam and press open.

    Note: Before moving on to fold and press the long edges of the bias strips, roughly lay each one out along the length of the neutral columns. Find the darkest piece (which should be the approximate center of the length) and lay it near the top of the lightest background square. Loosely create the loops as shown in the quilt by forming circles within each square and crossing them over each other where the squares are seamed together. This does not have to be perfect but helps ensure you have created a length of bias that is appropriate.

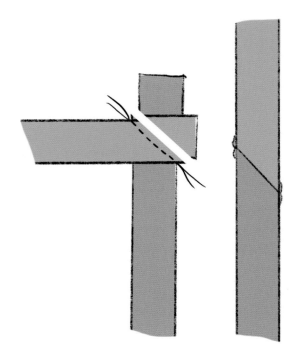

Fig. 1

- *If it seems a few inches too long, leave it as it is.*
- *If it seems 12" (30.5 cm) or more too long, trim off some length.*
- *If it seems a few inches too short, simply add another light strip at either end.*
- *If it seems much too short, cut the continuous length where you would like to add a color and value "at the area" where you would like (as only adding to the light end might give you more light than you want for the whole length).*

(continued)

Color Study Blueprint

3. Once each strip is to your liking and confirmed to be the right length, take your time, folding and pressing both long edges of the entire length of bias toward the wrong side of fabric by ¼" (6 mm).

Note: The next step might require more space to spread your project out than an ironing board can provide. I have a long homemade ironing mat that I made for my sewing counter where I worked on this project. Even if you don't have something similar, you may choose to press the strips on your bed or on top of a folded quilt on your dining room table.

4. Take your time placing one length of bias onto one of the vertical columns. Use the heat of the iron to stretch and curve the bias where needed as taught in Appliqué Adventures (page 54). Keep the widest point of the loops about ¾" to 1" (1.9 to 2.5 cm) away from the side edges of the background blocks. Once you are pleased with the shape of the design, overlap the ends over each other at the light end of the loop, and trim away excess. (When it comes time to stitch, you can tuck and blind-sew the overlapped end of the bias neatly so that it appears continuous.) If you have a favorite starch or spray finish, spray it on the loops and do a final pressing before glue tacking or straight pinning in place.

5. Choose whichever method you prefer to stitch the loops to the background. I used needle-turn appliqué by hand because I find these long and gentle curves so pleasant to sew and the background of a five-block column is never cumbersome to work with. If you choose to machine appliqué, take care not to stretch the fabric too much as you sew.

6. Repeat steps 4 and 5 with all four of the columns and press well.

7. Sew one column to the next in your desired arrangement, matching seam intersections and nesting seam allowances for a smooth finish.

8. Give the quilt top a final press before backing, quilting, and binding as desired.

▶ *Organizing fabrics by color*

CONVERSATIONS WITH GEORGIA QUILT

For this quilt, I decided to reference a master work—an age-old practice for artists. I chose to base my quilt on *Flower Abstraction* by Georgia O'Keeffe painted in 1924. My goal in creating this quilt was not replication, but rather to look deeply at the painting, and let it speak to me about its composition, shapes, lines, color, and overall feeling. I imagined showing Georgia my floral prints and her showing me her floral paintings. I got lost in this conversation and felt I learned something more about her that I could not have gathered from just viewing her work or from reading about her life. For the machine quilting, I wrote a sentence to her that I asked my quilter to stitch over and over across the quilt: "Dear Georgia, I dream of your simplicity, but know it must have also been chaos."

COLOR NOTES

Even if you decide that approaching something this improvisational is not quite your style, you can still celebrate a favorite work of art by using it to choose fabrics for your next quilt. While I did echo many of the soft peach, cream, gray, lavender, and pink tones of the artwork with highlights of yellow and punctuations of deep gray-green, at a certain point I began using colors truer to how I normally would. One of my favorite aspects of this quilt, in regards to color, is that it is just soft and neutral enough in its hues that the few exclamations of bright yellow and purple really speak up together.

Size: 60" × 76" (152.4 × 193 cm)

Building Block: Improvisational

Techniques: Machine Patchwork and Appliqué

Skill Level: Intermediate to Advanced

SUPPORTING YOUR IMPROVISATION

As this is a self-guided project, I am not giving you a pattern to follow; however, I will share as much as I can about my decision-making with this quilt and my own considerations when choosing fabrics. I hope this helps demystify my approach and maybe sparks some of your own ideas. I can't imagine trying to make a quilt like this without the help of a design wall, so you may want to find some space for one if you don't have one already

CHOOSING SIZE:

Knowing that this would be more of an "art" quilt that I would consider hanging on the wall, I decided to keep the scale (60" × 76" [152.4 × 193 cm]) nice and large but small enough to hang. And because I was borrowing the general composition of the inspiration painting, I also kept the portrait proportions (taller than wide) similar. You might choose to make a small quilt "study" first.

(continued)

CHOOSING FABRICS:

Creating a quilt where you might be a little less concerned with function than with visual appeal is a wonderful opportunity to play with some nontraditional quilt fabrics. It is a little difficult to tell from the image, but I used a few metallic linens as well as some velveteen pieces in my quilt. I also used fabrics that were a bit sheer intentionally so that some interesting color changes could happen as other fabrics passed underneath them. This idea points to how a sheer layer of paint might reveal the strokes that happened earlier.

Another very enjoyable endeavor was to look for fabrics in my studio that were imbued with some of the same feelings or even forms of the artwork. A good example of this in my quilt is the "Village Path" voile fabric in the upper right of the quilt. The wavy forms of the print reminded me of the scallop floral edge that some of the artist's forms share, so they felt appropriate to use.

CHOOSING TECHNIQUES:

Depending on the style of the artwork that you're using for inspiration, there may be styles of quilt blocks that would suit your attempt at honoring the art. Or at least there might be block styles that could be varied in some way to suit what you're trying to achieve.

Take, for instance, a color field painting. You could reproduce a Mark Rothko painting through almost any style of quilt block simply by selecting shades of fabric that move gradually around the space. Or a pixelated look at Monet's *Water Lilies* could be achieved through tiny square patchwork.

Part of what attracted me to *Flower Abstraction* was that I instantly saw the opportunity to recreate it with long strips of fabric and naturally shaped hand-cut scallops that could be slipped into those long seams. The overall V-shaped composition with some curves here and there felt quite doable. That is not to say that I didn't hit some roadblocks in deciding on my sequence along the way, but that is inevitable in an improvised pursuit. Taking your time and working through the hurdles, even if it

means stepping away for a few hours (or days), usually yields a clear path upon your return to the work.

Sketching your ideas onto graph paper, once you decide on general dimensions, can really help with this process. This simple act of drawing might conjure some lines or forms that then inform you with a style or technique of quilting. Do not worry about your drawing skills. You only need to understand your ideas.

In considering your inspiration piece, begin looking at it for its various elements of art (refresh your memory on those in chapter 1). Ask yourself, What quilting features or techniques might help retell this story? What are the key things that you love about the painting to begin with? If you can answer that with just a few words, you're well on your way to having a conversation with your favorite artist.

(continued)

MY SEWING & ASSEMBLY

The following is a general list of the order of my process in building this quilt. It will likely be different from yours; however, if you love the Georgia O'Keeffe painting as much as I do, perhaps you will be creating the next variation on a theme with me!

1. I printed out a photo of the painting to keep on the wall next to me while I selected fabrics. I took my time choosing the fabrics based on style, color, and mood for the quilt.

2. I then organized those fabrics into the basic features of the quilt, some of which I knew at an early stage. For instance, I knew what I was going to use for scallop petals and I generally knew what I was going to use for strip pieces. If I wasn't sure about a piece of fabric, it stayed in a separate pile that was organized simply by color.

3. I cut out an extra-wide piece of muslin that was roughly the desired finished dimensions of my overall quilt. I used my more-or-less final sketch as a plan to go by and roughly marked the muslin with a drawing tool. This became a bit of a road map for laying out the quilt. For example, I knew that I wanted the top of the main triangle to be a certain width and the bottom of it to be a certain width. I marked this quite literally onto the muslin and a few other shapes as well so that I could see how large each of the spaces were and therefore how much space I had to cover with fabrics. The illustration *(Fig. 1)* shows the general shapes that I broke the design into and built each one onto the muslin foundation.

4. One option of how to use a full-size muslin piece map is to cut out the pieces and use them for foundation piecing. (Refresh your memory on foundation piecing by reading through the Whippersnapper Block on page 47 where I used the tissue paper as the foundation.) I started by cutting out the large center triangle from the muslin map. I also cut it across the center to make it two pieces.

Fig. 1

5. Now that I was looking at a more defined shape (and not the whole quilt space), it was easier to begin laying out some of my fabrics and arrange some ideas of how I wanted the center triangle to take shape. I started with one floral triangle at the very top center of the quilt and used that as the first step in a foundation piecing process, making it bigger and longer gradually by adding hand-cut, imperfect strips. I also inserted some petals into those seams that I would appliqué down later. I felt quite excited once I had filled this whole piece and returned it to the quilt wall with the rest.

6. Next, I began to fill the lower narrow half of the center triangle, and I have a confession to make: I scrapped the first attempt. In fact, you can see my first attempt in the image of me working at the wall. Although I liked the assortment of fabrics, the lines were not angled enough. So I traced the overall triangle shape onto a new piece of muslin and started again. The second time I kept my eye on building the strips and shapes in a way that would create a more braided look with a sequence of points to emulate layered petals.

7. Each of these muslin foundation pieces became covered in fabric. In some cases, like the bold wide stripes of yellow and shades of lavender in the upper left, one single fabric covered the whole shape, so the muslin was just used as a pattern piece.

8. Once the top was assembled, I flipped it over and trimmed away as much muslin foundation between seams as I could to reduce the weight of the quilt. This is similar to cutting out background from appliqué. Pressing the quilt again actually helped it lay even smoother now that there was less foundation fabric. And a final view of the quilt actually encouraged me to add the top border of scallops. A true improvisational moment!

9. My quilt was not especially square at this stage, but I knew that it might further shift once quilted, so I resisted the urge to slice all the edges straight before sending for machine quilting. Being such a special project, it could be a nice opportunity to hand quilt as well.

ADJUSTING HER CROWN COLLAGE

I simply love when the worlds of patchwork and portraiture collide. I have made a few fabric portraits over the years, and this photo of my youngest daughter Mary Anna, taken in 2021, has been saved in my mind as one that I wanted to work with for a portrait. My children and I had moved out of our longtime family home to start over in a small historic cottage about twenty miles south of where they were brought up. To say the least, the move conjured a complex set of emotions, but the "crown" Mary Anna made for herself upon arrival to her new backyard was a reminder of how much I have been given in life. This portrait is a loving celebration of a time and place that I won't forget.

COLOR NOTES

I knew I wanted the types of fabrics I would use for this portrait to capture the sweetness of Mary Anna's age, but also the somewhat dramatic expression she is wearing. I chose small-scale floral prints, many from Liberty of London, but also richer and more saturated prints from my collections that punctuate the softer selections. I reimagined her dotted top as a blue floral print that carries a similar contrast to her skin tones for the image. Finally, I chose to seal her collaged silhouette onto a piece of linen from France that was gifted to me by my friend Lorraine in Adelaide, South Australia. The juxtaposition of Mary Anna's pose against the Victorian–style paper dolls is unique and compelling.

Size: 48" × 48" (121.9 × 121.9 cm)

Technique: Collage

Skill Level: Beginner to Advanced

FABRICS

Inspiration image or photograph

Tracing paper

Pencil and fine-tip permanent marker

Steam-a-Seam 2® or Pellon® 805 (two to three times more than your desired image size)

Muslin (or a sheer woven cotton) in the final desired size of your image (plus a few inches)

Single background fabric in desired size (with enough extra to stretch around canvas if desired)

Assorted scraps of fat quarters in desired colors for collage (lawn or voile recommended)

CREATING YOUR IMAGE

In deciding on an image to use for your portrait, keep in mind it does not have to be a portrait at all. You could choose a still life, a landscape, or even a portrait of your pet. The key to a good image is that it is clear enough and defined enough that you're able to discern various areas of color and value to break it out into parts for reassembling with fabric.

(continued)

1. The first step is to translate the image into line work. If you're skilled in digital media, then you might prefer to make your drawing digitally as a layer over the original image (I used the Procreate app on my iPad). But a paper and pencil process works as well. Print the image large enough so that you can make a clear drawing; at least 8.5" × 11" (21.6 × 27.9 cm) would be a good size. Tape the print to a tabletop and then tape tracing paper over it to keep it still. Pencil the silhouette as well as different sections of the image. If it is a portrait, imagine the places where you would want to use a different shade of fabric and outline those. For instance, I knew that darker nostrils and cheek highlights would be different colors in my portrait. Refer to the illustration showing the line drawing over the image of Mary Anna. I have not detailed every last feature, but in some places I have consolidated shapes. For instance, in her hair and lash line, the shapes are more general. *Don't forget: The lines need to form shapes so that they can be turned into templates.*

2. Once you're pleased with the drawing, go over the lines you want to keep with a fine-tip permanent marker to make smooth edges. Again, you will be simplifying the shapes either somewhat or greatly for your desired outcome.

3. Reproduce your final line drawing at a larger scale. There are plenty of printers that can do this for you, even at a large scale. I used my local printer to reproduce my small drawing all the way up to 36" (91.4 cm) square. It was only a few dollars per copy, so I went ahead and got two copies to be safe.

4. Tape your full-scale drawing onto a smooth surface, layer the muslin over the top of it, and secure it with more tape. You should be able to see the lines through the fabric well, but if not, you might need to draw over the copy with a thicker permanent marker. The other option is to tape both onto a large window to increase visibility. Redraw the lines once more onto the muslin. I find it best to do this with a sharp pencil. This muslin is the base layer, or "piece map," if you will, to which all the pieces will be fused.

(continued)

My original photograph of Mary Anna felt like a magical moment.

I traced the image to capture the key sections of color and light.

PREPARING TEMPLATES AND FABRICS

1. The printed piece map (paper copy) you just traced is now your puzzle that needs to be cut out. But first, if you enjoy coloring, you may want to take the time and a nice big set of colored pencils to lightly color in the shapes of the drawing to help you plan your fabric color choices. You can refer back to your original photograph, and don't forget, you get to update colors however you wish. You could also color-code the pieces with notes or numbers and make a corresponding fabric color key. Either way, choose some method to mark on the right side of each shape in the paper piece map.

2. You can now begin carefully cutting out each shape in the piece map. Here is where I really appreciated having a second copy of the print, because you will have somewhere to keep the paper shapes that have not yet been translated to fabric.

3. If you have selected all of your fabrics, or at least have some fabrics you're sure about, you can go ahead and seal some of the fusible onto the wrong side of the fabric. For now, leave the backing paper on.

Anna Maria's Blueprint Quilting

CUT AND ASSEMBLE COLLAGE

1. As you make decisions about which fabrics to use for each shape, use the paper pieces as templates to cut from the fabrics. Make sure the marked side of the paper template and the right side of the fabric are both facing up as you hold them together and cut. (Keep in mind that if you haven't put fusible on the back of all your fabrics yet, you may choose to do this in scraps as you go. Make sure the fusible piece is larger than the template piece you will cut from it.) Depending on how irregular the shape is, it might be easiest to trace it onto the fabric and then cut it out. Once the fabric piece is cut, remove the fusible backing paper and lay the shape onto the muslin in its matching position (Fig. 1).

2. Press the shape in place with the heat of an iron to fuse it to the muslin piece map, or you can wait until you have a cluster of shapes adjacent to one another all cut out and make sure they fit nicely together before fusing. I think waiting until you have several pieces in place before fusing is a bit more efficient and helpful in the process of color choices. I changed my mind about the color or print of a few pieces here and there and simply cut new pieces. Be sure to press gently with the iron and make sure none of the pieces shift.

3. Continue the process of cutting, placing, and pressing until your image has been rebuilt with fabric.

4. You might like the look of the image against a simple muslin background, and if so, your project is complete. You can now decide whether to stretch it onto a canvas and have it framed or frame it into a large embroidery hoop.

5. (Optional) If you would like to seal it to a different background, you can now press the fusible product onto the whole background of the portrait silhouette. Carefully cut out the silhouette, peel off the fusible backing paper, and press it to your desired background. Stretch around a canvas or frame as desired.

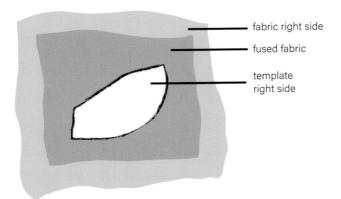

fabric right side

fused fabric

template right side

Fig. 1

Scan to watch a tutorial.

TEMPLATES

These templates are used to create the quilt blocks referenced in this book. You can trace them onto paper or template plastic, photocopy them, or download them using the QR code provided, then cut them out. When downloading and printing out, just be sure to choose 100 percent on your printer so that the size reflects the size on these pages.

Scan to download the templates.

The dotted lines with the Light Ray templates mean that those shapes are a larger size than the book size would allow. Therefore, join the dotted lines together with tape once cut out to create the full-size template before using to cut fabric. You can also trace the two parts of the same piece to create one whole piece.

The dotted line on the Extra Large Dresden template only needs to be added to the Large Dresden template when you need that extra large size. The Large Dresden template can also be used as it is.

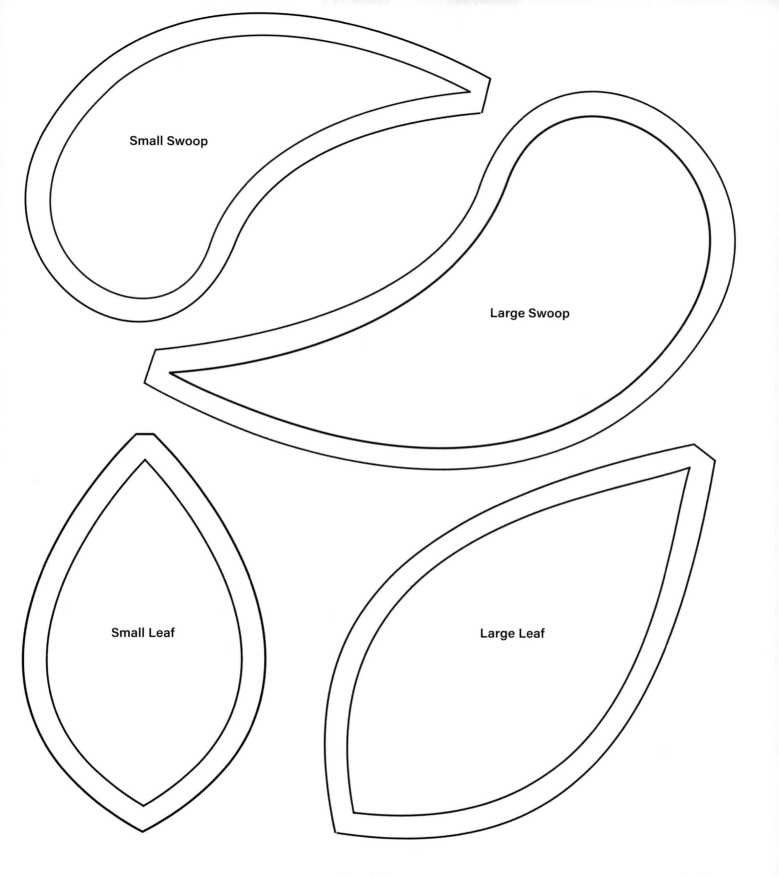

Small Swoop

Large Swoop

Small Leaf

Large Leaf

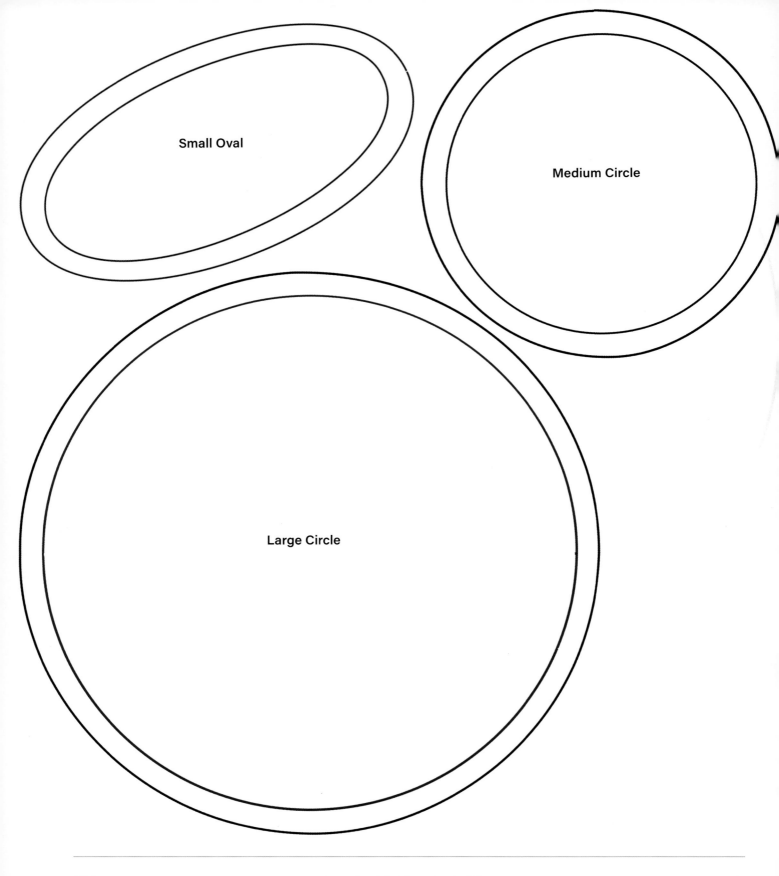

Small Oval

Medium Circle

Large Circle

Anna Maria's Blueprint Quilting

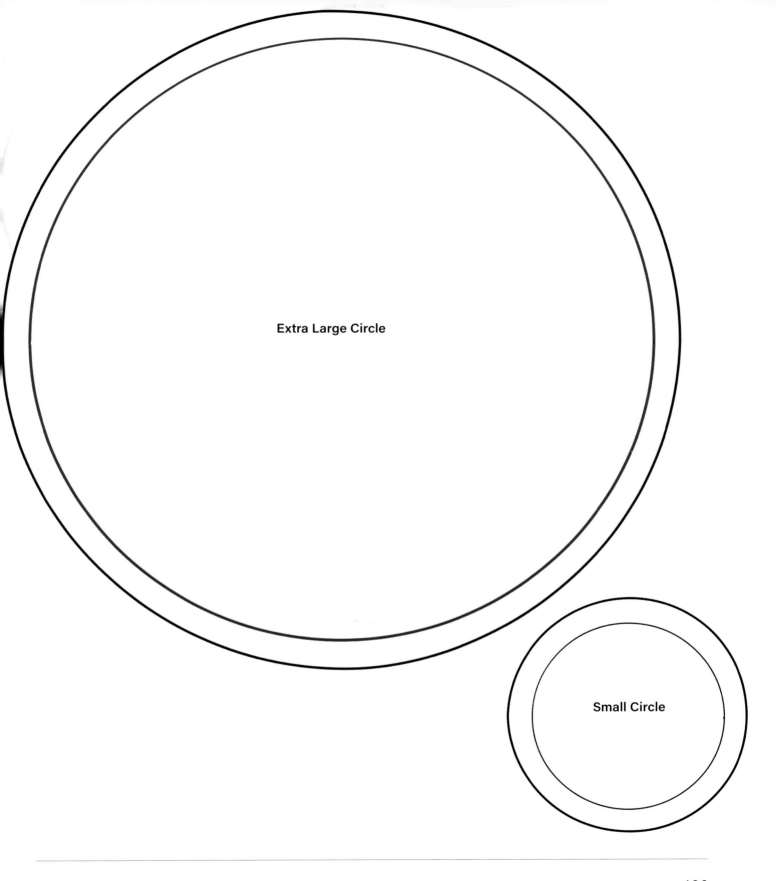

Extra Large Circle

Small Circle

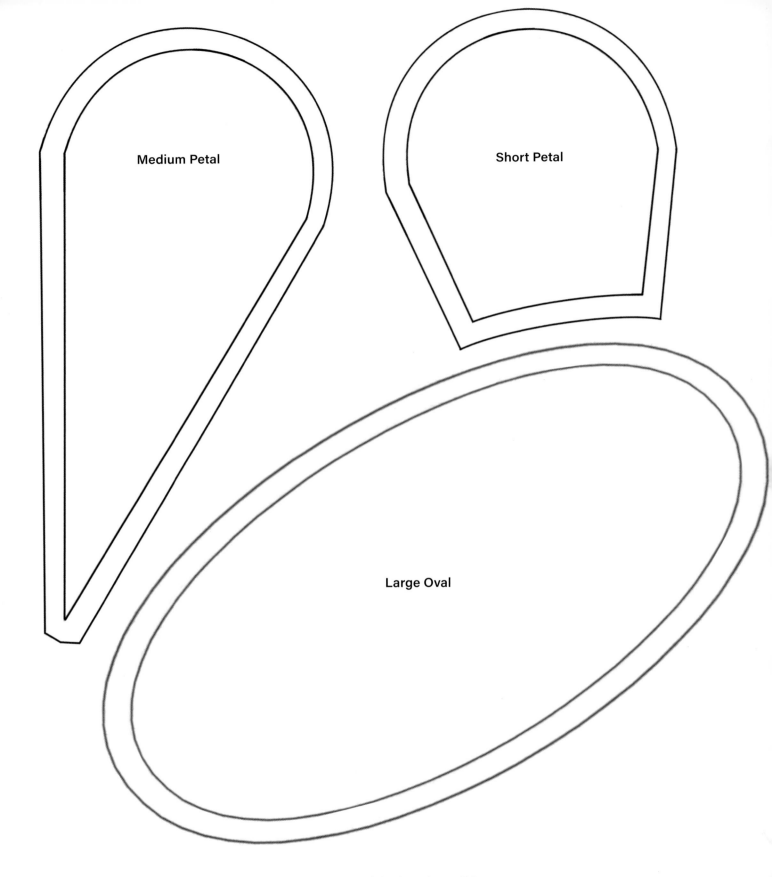

Medium Petal

Short Petal

Large Oval

Anna Maria's Blueprint Quilting

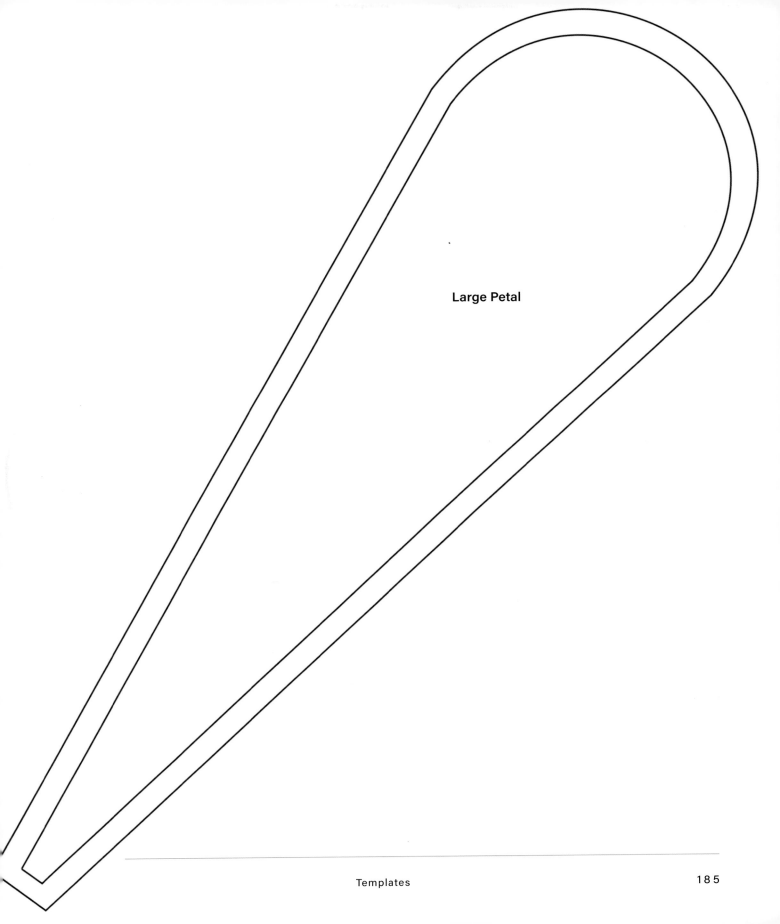

Large Petal

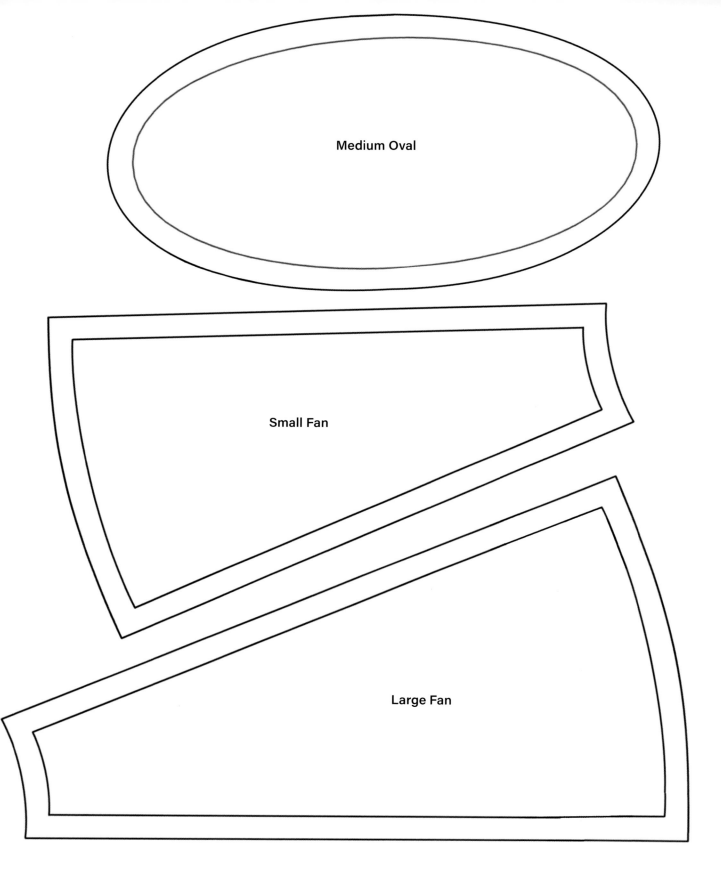

Medium Oval

Small Fan

Large Fan

Anna Maria's Blueprint Quilting

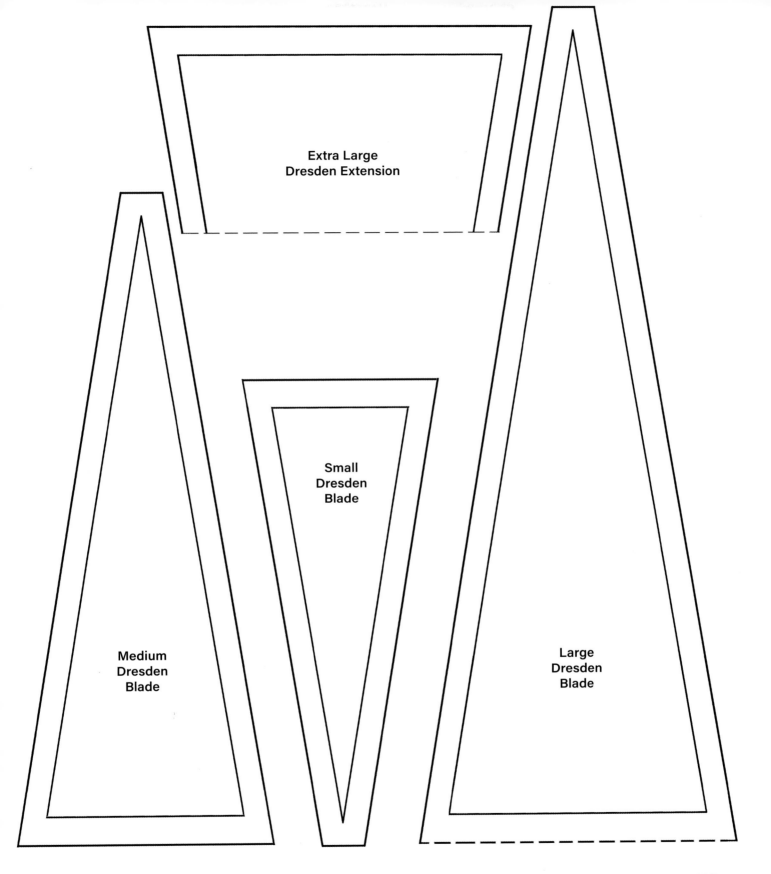

Extra Large
Dresden Extension

Small
Dresden
Blade

Medium
Dresden
Blade

Large
Dresden
Blade

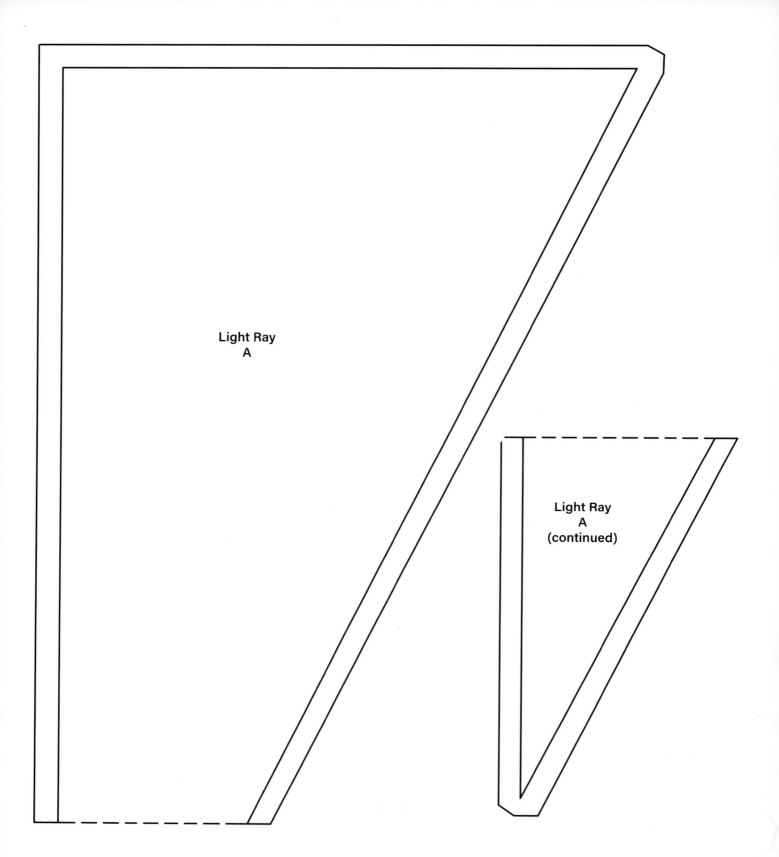

Light Ray
A

Light Ray
A
(continued)

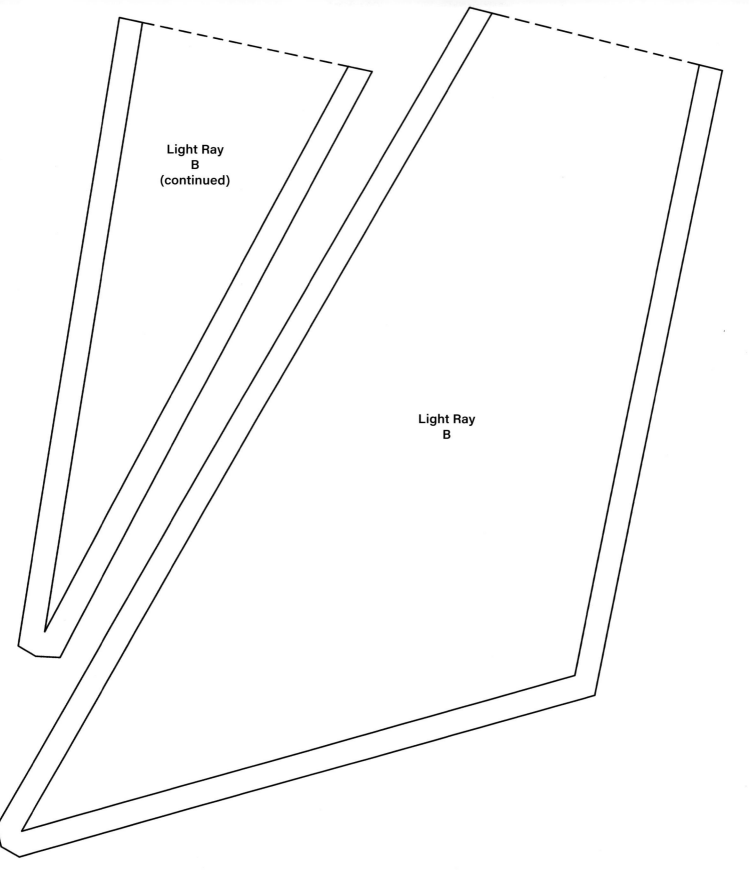

Light Ray
B
(continued)

Light Ray
B

ABOUT THE AUTHOR

Having grown up in a creative home, **Anna Maria Parry** earned an honors BFA in drawing from the University of Tennessee in 1995 before opening a small clothing shop with her mother the same year. Designing and sewing a clothing label while managing a shop primed her for a career in textiles and small business. After transitioning to freelance partnerships with various companies, her art was discovered by Donna Wilder, the founder of FreeSpirit fabrics. Since her first fabric collection debuted in 2005, she has designed hundreds of illustrative fabric prints that have inspired crafters and quilters around the globe. She is now the design director for Anna Maria Textiles (a division of Northcott) and sharing her distinctive quilt-making process has taken her all over the world to teach and lecture. *Blueprint Quilting* is Anna Maria's fourth book, and she self-publishes an ongoing collection of sewing, quilting, and needlework patterns at annamariaparry.com. Anna Maria has been a guest on the *Martha Stewart Show* and has been featured in numerous publications such as *Artist's Magazine* and *Cottage Journal*. She lives with her husband and family between Franklin, Tennessee, and Sydney, Australia.

INDEX